It Could Have Gone Either Way

the times I Almost Died

by

Robert C.A. Goff

Dreamsplice
Christiansburg, Virginia

It Could Have Gone Either Way: the times I almost died

Dreamsplice
3462 Dairy Road
Christiansburg, VA 24073

www.dreamsplice.com/books

Cover design by Robert C.A. Goff, Copyright © 2022 by Dreamsplice

ISBN 13: 978-1-7333979-8-8

Library of Congress Control Number: 2022911984

First Edition: July 2022

Contents

Dedication

To my grandfather, Menashe Amato, given no middle name, to my father, Morris Amato, also given no middle name, and to my son, Micah Menashe Amato Goff, who carries the burden of my having given him two middle names that commemorate them both.

Robert Charles Amato Goff

Other Works by Robert C.A. Goff

Fantasy-fiction by Robert C.A. Goff
> **Ternaria: Legacy of a Careless Age**

Science-fiction by Robert C.A. Goff
> **Impact Mitigation** and other Science-fiction
> Short Stories

Non-fiction by Robert C.A. Goff
> **In the Ozone:** collected essays, poems and
> non-fiction
> **Climbing Out:** Grand Canyon Hikes 1997-2006
> **Just Walking Home:** AT Hikes 1996-2013
> **How to Read a US Roadmap**
> **Grow Your Own Cigars:** growing, curing and
> finishing tobacco at home
> **Blend Your Own Pipe Tobacco:** 52 recipes with
> 52 color labels
> **Ninety More Pipe Blends:** 90 more recipes with
> 90 color labels
> **The Cigar Artistry of Marc Langanes:**
> torcedor and photographer

Fantasy-fiction by Robert C.A. Goff and Micah M.A. Goff

The Counterspell Chronicle
> **Counterspell: Guardian of the Ruins**
> **Counterspell: The Second Law**
> **Counterspell: Age of Fool**s [upcoming]

Preface

This book originated as a curious list that I began about ten years ago, recalling the half-dozen times I nearly died. It expanded. The more I considered the details of my life, the more instances arose. I suspect that every person who has never been directly involved in military combat, and lived over a half-century could assemble a similarly lengthy list.

Although there are many similarities of this book with a memoir or autobiography, these elements are included to set the context of each of my near-death experiences. I have ignored many of my sins and shortcomings. I have ignored many of my successes and admirable moments. In mentioning others, by first name only, I have attempted to avoid past grievances and facile, accusatory labels. I've tried my best to recall the dates correctly, and to not embellish the tales for literary purposes. It's all true.

I have left out numerous old friends and others I have cared deeply about. They were not contextually associated with my having almost died. The book moves along chronologically, but only in the form of brief vignettes. Place this copy on your toilet tank for...episodic...reading.

R.C.A.G

1. Bullet at the Center of the Grill

1952

I didn't waste any time. I nearly succeeded in getting myself killed before my fourth birthday. Most of the circumstances of this event remain a blur. My memories from age 3 or 4 consist of brief vignettes, with few points of reference. But my vivid image of the bullet at the center of the grill is deeply imprinted.

Our two-story red brick home in Atlanta rested on a modest lawn which sloped abruptly in a six-foot descent to the sidewalk, beyond which a four-foot-wide strip of grass and mature silver maple trees separated the sidewalk from the curbing of Yorkshire Road. This was a neighborhood of 1930s vintage homes along a road with only occasional vehicle traffic.

For a small child, a six-foot slope of grass was both a challenge and a rich source of fun. This day Ronnie, my older brother (by 15 months) and I were taking turns racing directly down the grassy hill to the sidewalk. I believe the game was to see how quickly you could stop, once you reached the sidewalk.

For reasons long forgotten, I decided to continue racing beyond the sidewalk and the grass strip, and all the way to the curbing on the opposite side of Yorkshire Road. Made this run repeatedly, running back up the grassy hill after each excursion.

While obliviously sprinting into the road on one pass, I was halted by the peripheral vision of a large object to my left. As I turned my head to look, I discovered a bright chrome, circular bullet as large as my head, less than a foot from my face. [Since 3 and 4 year old children "sprint" by bending forward, rather than running upright, the height of the bullet above the street could well be less than my indelible memory of it.] The bullet was the center decoration of the grill of a car. Its bumper was even closer. A dark maroon car, almost dark purple.

I don't recall a horn sounding, or anyone shouting. I do recall turning back to my side of Yorkshire Road, and running up onto the curb. That was my last oblivious run into a street for the remainder of my life.

Years later, I learned that the bullet at the center of the grill was the distinctive identifier of a 1949 Ford. The bullet didn't poke out, like the later Studebakers. So the car that didn't kill me was younger than me. I have no recollection of having seen or even having looked at the driver. It was just a car.

2. Stabbed in the Back

1954

Our house in Atlanta was built during the 1930s. In an exterior wall alongside the driveway was a square, cast iron door. In the past, a coal chute attached to the interior of that door, and led into the coal bin, for shoveling coal to feed the coal furnace which provided convection-driven, central heating into each room in the house, via its octopus like, round ducts that emerged from its top. These ducts were circular in cross-section, and insulated by several inches of asbestos. The seven-foot diameter, squat, cylindrical coal furnace was also entombed in thick asbestos. Early on, I learned that I could pee into the floor vent of the bedroom I shared with Ronnie, and it would just vanish forever.

By the time we had moved into the house (when I was two), that same furnace was still there, but had been converted to use natural gas. We could open its cast iron, coal door, and see a circle of gas flames inside it. Since the basement was mostly unfinished, and supplied with only one or two hanging light bulbs, the furnace located near the bottom of the wooden, basement steps, cast a deep shadow behind it. I could walk back there, but seldom chose to. It was a mysterious, spooky place.

From the time I was about three, I can recall a recurring dream. In that dream, I stood at the verge of the furnace shadow. From deep within that shadow, a beast would slowly emerge—not leaping at me, but steadily moving closer. Sometimes the beast was a massive hippopotamus; sometimes a huge, black wolf. I would always awaken with a sense of impending danger.

My baby sister, Lynn, was born in 1953, when I was 4½. Once she was old enough to kind of hang on, I would carry her about the house from time to time, with her sitting on my hip. We would tour one room after another, as I explained the world to her.

One day in late 1954, I decided to take Lynn for a tour of the basement. We did not go into the shadow of the furnace. Instead I carried her on my hip as I walked along the top of a cinder block retaining wall that circled the interior of a solid dirt deck that abutted the house foundation all around. There was scattered debris in my path, to step over: stuff that three boys might leave haphazardly tossed out the way.

At one point, where the coal bin used to be, there were loose cinder blocks formed into a rude stairway. As I began to descend, still carrying Lynn, I lost my balance.

I clearly remember that slow motion event. I would be falling forward onto the loose cinder blocks, landing on top of Lynn. In an instant decision, while in mid-fall, I rotated my body, so that Lynn would fall on top of me.

I missed the cinder blocks, landing directly on my back, Lynn on top of me. The landing was not too painful. I set Lynn onto her feet, on the paved part of the basement floor. As I sat up, I could feel something pulling at my back—about mid-chest. At the sound of a heavy hunk of lumber striking the floor behind be, I turned to see a ½"x6" plank lying just where I had landed. A bloody, 10 penny nail stuck straight out of it.

After an emergency visit to the doctor, and x-rays, the verdict was in. Given my thin physique, that 10 penny nail had punctured deeply into the right paraspinous muscle, missing my lung as well as the right atrium of my heart. A half-inch to either side would have poked a hole in my heart or my right lung.

In the end, the wound was just scrubbed and flushed well. A big band-aid was applied. As punishment for being so careless, I had to get a tetanus shot.

A year before I incurred this injury, Queen Elizabeth II was crowned. My scar is still there.

3. Flash Gordon in the Fuse Box

1950s

Many carnival rides provide a "minimum height" gauge near the entrance. If you are less than that minimum height, then you are not allowed to climb onto the ride. Flash Gordon in the Fuse Box offered a built-in minimum height requirement. You had to be tall enough to reach it from the steep, wooden steps that descended into the basement of our house.

Since children seldom quantify their stature—"Oh my, you're getting taller, Bobby."—this event likely occurred in the mid-1950s. By 7 to 9 years old, most kids are not stupid enough to give this a try. [Of course, we have to remember the stupid "challenges" that have become widespread on social media during the 21st century. Children certainly old enough to realize their stupidity attempt them nonetheless.]

During the 1950s, home electrical fuse boxes did not have circuit breakers sporting hefty, plastic switches. Instead, when the thin metal door of the fuse box was swung open, one saw two columns of brass-colored, screw-in sockets, each accommodating a solid, 1-inch, circular glass fuse with a flat window for viewing the continuity of a silvery metal strip inside. They screwed in like a light bulb. When a fuse was "blown", the metal strip was broken, and sometimes sooty smudges were left inside the flat window—time to change the fuse to a new one of a similar amperage rating. But each of those brass-colored sockets was capable of transmitting 120 volts of the full amperage served by the electric company to that house. That is comparable to the total amperage of the house's power line outdoors.

In the absence of social influencers during 1950s, older siblings and cousins handily filled that role. In my encounter with Flash

Gordon in the fuse box, I cannot clearly recall who proposed the challenge to me. The fact that I can recall anything at all is a testament to my having both survived the challenge, and its fortunate setting of requiring me to stand on dry, wooden steps in order to reach it.

For unknown reasons, there was always an empty, brass colored socket in our fuse box, even though an unused circuit in the box could always be safely hidden behind a saved, blown-out fuse. "Stick your thumb in there, and you'll see Flash Gordon. Really."

The action of making a fist to get my thumb to stick out meant that when the inevitable jolt of electricity zapped my thumb, its resulting muscular spasm instantly withdrew my thumb. My skin was not burned, or injured in any way. I survived due to luck.

My vivid recollection of Flash Gordon in the fuse box, and my retrospective realization of its danger yielded a singular effect in my adulthood. When my son (now with kids of his own) was still crawling on all fours, at our 1903 vintage brown shingle house in Berkeley, California, and reached for a plug socket on the living room wall, I intentionally slapped his hand hard enough for it to remain reddened for a while. It was the only time in my life when I struck him. I never spanked him.

4. Panama City Sand Bar

1957

While my father was still living, we used to spend a week each summer at Panama City Beach, on the Gulf coast of Florida's panhandle. Sometimes other families from our Atlanta community would join us, and sometimes we would make the trip with just a cousin joining the six of us in our cream-colored 1951 Chrysler sedan. On some of those vacation trips, we would stay in a cottage that sat right at the top of the slope of the bright white beach, separated from it by only a paved sidewalk.

There was no TV in the cottage back then. But we always had a radio handy. I recall the Republican National Convention nominating Ike Eisenhower for his second term, and threats of hurricanes blaring during evenings spent there. On several occasions, I sat outside after dark, watching miles-wide lightning storms far out over the water.

Our family photos are overloaded with Panama City backgrounds, chronicling the our procession from toddlers to middle-school-aged kids. And the tans! My father's Sephardic heritage gifted his skin with the ability to acquire the very deepest of suntans, while my Kentucky Methodist mother tended to freckle and burn easily. Everybody glistened with Coppertone tanning lotion from start to finish.

At nine years old, I was a somewhat runty kid, but a strong and confident swimmer, both above and beneath the water. In Panama City, I discovered that if I squinted under water, then I could see what was down there, without my eyes stinging too much from the brine. Some summers, the water was filled with nests of floating seaweed, which also cluttered the beach. Other summers, it was inundate with gelatinous, colorless little jellyfish, that I never actually saw in the water, but easily spotted littering the sand, like a teaspoon of transparent jelly. They did not sting.

The sandbars near the shore seemed to change their location every year. One summer I could swim just a short stretch of adult-depth water before I could once again stand with my head above all but the highest waves. Then I would look back at the sweep of the beach, and its long row of beach-front rental cottages.

In the summer of 1957, I swam from the beach beneath the water, looking for the sandbar. It seemed farther out than I had remembered. I surfaced for air several times, but never thought to look back. At last, I planted my feet on a rise of reassuring sand, popped up my head, and turned around. I clearly recall my astonishment at how far I was from the beach. I could see dark people against white sand, but just barely. In retrospect, that sandbar was 150 to 200 yards out.

After resting there, bobbing up and down with the gentle waves, while watching a helicopter pass overhead going one direction, then the opposite direction, I swam back—this time above the water. I told nobody about my excursion, for fear of being reprimanded.

That evening, in our cottage, there was a discussion about the shark problem. It had become serious enough, one adult speculated, that they had begun to fly helicopters across the shoreline, to patrol the beach.

Turning Over The Engine

1960

This is a sidebar, since my life was never endangered by the event. But I was an immediate witness. The potential victim in this instance is my eldest brother, Richard. At the time, he was either in 11th Grade, or had just finished it. He was already an experienced auto mechanic, specializing in beat-up old cars and high decibel muffler modifications.

This day, he was working on the flat-head V-8 engine of a 1949 Hudson, if I recall. Not leaning over the fender, but worked on the engine that was sitting all by itself directly on the pavement of the driveway. Its host car sat parked on the street, engineless.

Our driveway originated at the two-car garage in the corner of our back yard, ascended the steep slope to almost the level of our front yard, then dipped downward again to Yorkshire Road. Almost at the crest of that driveway hill, our 1959 Plymouth Belvedere had been parked. "Almost" meaning it was on a slope.

"Get out of the way!", Richard yelled to me.

When I looked up, I watched Richard jump toward the Plymouth's rear bumper, attempting to stop its motion with his extended arms. Like magic, the Plymouth lifted him a short distance into the air, tossing him backwards, and still in its path.

He nimbly leapt to his feet and retreated toward the open garage, where I fully expected the Plymouth to crush him against the rear wall.

But the flat-head V8, resting directly on the pavement, in the center of the driveway, was in the path of the vengeful Plymouth. The car, its speed accelerating by gravity alone, smacked into the flat-head. The Plymouth's rear end abruptly rose up into the air, as the massive hunk of cast iron rolled beneath it, partially crushing the gas tank. Then the Plymouth stopped.

5. Calama Fireworks: a Pine Panel Chemistry Lab

1960

When my father converted the unfinished attic of our Atlanta house into a bedroom for my two older brothers and me, it occupied most of the available space, spanning the full width of the house. Its new bathroom, complete with sink, toilet, tub and built-in laundry hamper, took up only a small chunk of the abundant floor space. The remainder was a huge, open bedroom, with three widely separated single beds sculpted beneath the eaves. Every vertical surface—walls, closet doors, etc. was constructed of ¾-inch, tongue and groove, knotty pine paneling. Ronnie's built-in bunk was located at one end, mine at the opposite end, and Richard's was situated directly across from me. Each of the bunks rested above storage compartments, and occupied the sloping space beneath the eaves. Even that sloping ceiling was pine panel. Our dressers, each with a fold-down desk, were also built into the walls. A double fan rested in the window at each end of the long room, to keep it cool during the Georgia summers.

Pine paneling, in the care of three boys is always doomed. We put up a dart board that used real darts. All the misses left a halo of punctures surrounding the target. Random nails were pounded in wherever they could conveniently hang something.

We had chemistry sets. But Richard created an actual laboratory counter by placing a 4' x 8' sheet of heavy, unfinished plywood over two saw horses, and situated it beside his bed. As a high school junior, he could go into a chemical supply house in Atlanta, and easily purchase explosive chemicals and related ingredients "for agricultural use". No questions asked. Stuff to make gunpowder—no problem.

He and a high school friend decided to manufacture fireworks. To grind up the chunky, dry chemicals, he used a tiny 15 or 20 watt incandescent light bulb—just the bulb—as a pestle, and one of our mother's Fiestaware teacups as a mortar. Close to the pine panel wall, his laboratory counter was lined with assorted cartons, some the size of a carton of Morton salt, others in smaller cardboard cylinders and in jars.

One of the products of this lab was a collection of various sizes of "pinwheels", made from metal ointment tins with canted nail holes poked into the sides, then taped over, with a single fuse dangling. Inside the tins was a blend of explosive powder, aluminum dust, and sometimes bits of magnesium ribbon. Hand-written on the top label, it said, "Calama Fireworks." When one of these miraculous pinwheels was set down on the pavement outside, and its fuse lit with a match, it would send out two tight jets of flame, one on either side, the pinwheel would begin to spin rapidly, then it would suddenly zoom high into the air, spraying a trail of brightly glowing, sparkling exhaust. Once its combustibles were expended, the somewhat charred ointment tin would drop back to earth. What fun!

Some of the chemicals were sensitive to friction. Pack it into something with tiny bits of rock, and throw it against a hard surface, and it would explode. Mortar, pestle, grinding, friction....

One afternoon, when Richard was working at his lab, and I was building a gadget on the floor with my Erector Set, something on the lab bench ignited, and set the plywood surface on fire. I don't recall what triggered the lab fire or how Richard extinguished it before the abundant, nearby explosives joined in. But I clearly recall the huge, pine paneled room filling with thick, acrid smoke, and the window fan being switched on to clear it away.

6. Bicycling to Stone Mountain

1961

I had an awesome 24" bicycle of no recognizable brand. Just one speed. No dainty, "English" 3-speed, with timid, tucked-in handlebars. It was a beast! I had modified it by replacing the street tires with fat ones, which necessitated removing both fenders. My wire basket on the front was supported by the hefty, solid aluminum struts that once supported a folding lawn chair. And of course, the chain guard had to go. Young adolescents seldom consider the possibility of mud and water spraying up from both tires, or the risk of catching one's trouser hem between the greasy chain and the pedal sprocket. But I thought my customized bike looked ferocious.

Ronnie and I (I don't remember his bike at all) bicycled all over the place. Sometimes we rode all the way to downtown Atlanta, sometimes to distant, new shopping malls.

Once beyond the immediate Atlanta area, the Georgia roads were still the same two-lane, poorly maintained, meandering blacktop highways from the 1930s. Their lanes were barely wide enough for two trucks to pass one another in opposite directions. Though faintly marked with a centerline, Georgia roads back then were not painted with a side stripe, indicating the outer margin of the road (something you hardly notice as a driver today, until there isn't one). There were no shoulders. The ragged edge of the asphalt would drop a couple inches to the steeply sloping road bed, drained by a weed-filled ditch.

To me, growing up in Atlanta during the 1950s, Stone Mountain was just a gigantic rock with an unfinished, enormous relief carving on its vertical face. I failed to read its racial and political implications. The distance from our home on Yorkshire Road to Stone

Mountain is only about 15 miles. Ronnie and I agreed that 15 miles wasn't too bad, and decided to bicycle out there on a warm, sunny day.

One aspect of our planned excursion that I did not consider was that a 15 mile bike ride in one direction was only half the trip. Another overlooked aspect was that bicycling along that highway would be just a shave short of suicidal. Yet a third failure was to have not realized that both Ronnie and I should carry along some water to drink. Everywhere that we had ever biked through had some kind of water fountain or spigot. At least we planned it as an all-day excursion.

I don't recall stopping anywhere other than at our destination, and successfully finding drinking water at a water fountain (Whites Only) outside the Stone Mountain Museum. I also cannot recall whether or not we expended more energy climbing up that daunting, bald rock. Having visited there with several school groups over the years, the climbing and the views from the top are a bit of a blur now.

In 1961, the relief carving was incomplete. The bottom half of it had not yet been carved. That wouldn't happen for another decade. The visitor center displayed drawings of what it would eventually look like.

What I most clearly recall is our return trip. Fifteen more miles along that narrow highway in the late afternoon. My clothes were saturated with sweat. My thigh muscles quivered at the exertion. But my focus was firmly held by that broken edge of asphalt, along which I pedaled my bike. Cars whizzed past at 60 mph, only inches from the tip of my handlebars. And the trucks...the trucks with their extended side mirrors. I still have memories of the trucks. Dozens of times during that return ride, I could feel an extended side-mirror passing so close to my head that it would wag my left ear in its wake. The sudden blasting of truck air horns at least drew my elbows to my ribs. But there was nowhere to go. It was simply not possible for me or Ronnie to get out of the way. Improving that old highway wouldn't happen for another decade as well.

7. Constitutional Meets Revolutionary

1962

My father died in the summer of 1959, while on the operating table for open-heart surgery. They had replaced a bum aortic valve. By 1961, my mother had remarried, and the two of them had chosen to change our last names (actually append a fourth name). Then we moved from Atlanta to Warminster, Pennsylvania.

I went from being a marginally delinquent, Atlanta pre-teen, casual Sephardic Jew to being a new kid at school for 8th grade, in Yankie territory. And the step-son of a Baptist Preacher. New start in a new place, new religion, new name, new accents, new social expectations, a changing body, and no friends.

I had always been recognized as a bright underachiever. When I arrived at William Tennent Jr. High, my school records and standardized tests from Atlanta would not follow me there until after the first semester had ended. So I had the genuine joy of being placed into the "vocational training" path. I took wood shop, machine shop, metal shop, in addition to the flat-out boring English, math and social studies classes.

During my first weeks at the new school in the new land, while walking down the crowded school hallway, an older boy plucked the ball-point pen out of my shirt pocket. All boys wore button up shirts with a front pocket back then. And they all had to carry a ball-point pen somewhere.

"Giv it back!", I shouted.

He instead tossed it to one of his buddies. They proceeded to play the time-honored game of "keep-away".

"Giv it back!", I shouted again, more loudly. "It's mine!"

Suddenly, a chorus of dozens of students began to chant, "It's mine. It's mine," in the most exaggerated Southern accent imaginable.

With a sinking realization, I saw that the chorus was accurately reflecting how I sounded to them, with their Philadelphia accents (drink wooder, play bawl). In that moment of revelation, I became a student of colloquial accents, and committed to never again sounding like I came from Georgia. And I never again did.

One of my first friends, Stan, lived only a block away. I lived on Revolutionary Way. He lived just around the corner and up the hill on Constitutional Drive. That first winter there was the first real opportunity I had experienced to hop onto a Flexible-Flier sled, and careen down a deeply snow covered street with an underlayment of thick ice. The speed was amazing, prone and head-first. Even faster was if a friend, say Stan, pushed me at the top of the hill, and then plopped on top of me, adding his mass to the momentum equation.

The only hitch in the fun was that, heading downhill from Stan's house on Constitutional, the road curved to the left where it intersected Revolutionary. You had to make that turn at high-speed, head first. Otherwise, you might hit the concrete curbing at the end of Revolutionary. Beyond that curbing a clear stretch of deep, soft snow extended for at least 15 feet, before that home's rail fence stood.

It was the best and fastest run, with Stan stooping on the back, his hands griping my waist tightly. The runners of the Flexible-Flier jumped out of their icy rut, and halted instantly on the concrete curbing. Both Stan and I were somersaulted high into air. We landed on our backs in the deep, soft snow. Whew! When I sat up, I saw that my snow boots were almost touching the lowest rail of the solidly built fence.

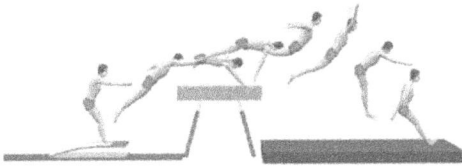

8. Attempting the Hecht Vault

1966

William Tennent High School was a place of transformation for me. By my second semester, my school records from Atlanta had finally arrived. I was placed into the advanced, college prep curriculum. Suddenly, for the first time in my life, not a single course was boring. I loved every class. I joined the Choral Club, and in 9th grade, tried out for the varsity (and only) gymnastics team. When the final list of students who made the cut—who would be allowed to continue in gymnastics—was posted on the locker room bulletin board, all of the names were written in firm, black ink. At the bottom of the list, written in pencil, it said, "Bob Goff." I had made it, but only as an afterthought. That year, still only in 9th grade, I earned my varsity letter—a huge, black and white chenille 'T', specializing in "all around." I also competed in pole vaulting in the spring, and tied the Jr. High record on the very same day that one of my teammates broke that record. I earned a much smaller 'T' for pole vaulting.

The following fall, now in 10th grade, I was shocked into profound memories of my friends and classmates and where I was. President Kennedy had been assassinated on November 22, 1963.

Every classroom had a closed-circuit TV up in a front corner, mostly for watching the principal drone on about the morning's announcement. That day, it went live to news coverage, and stayed on all day long. The moment struck so deeply, that even now, at the age of 74, I briefly sob as I type this. I was in my Euclidean Geometry class.

But by early 1964 (part-way into the second semester of my 10th grade year), our family moved again, from Warminster to Upper

Darby, Pennsylvania. New home, new school (which did not have a gymnastics team) and again, no friends.

My experience at William Tennent had taught me how to make new friends, and so I did. But I missed my friends from Warminster, and occasionally took the bus, then the commuter train into Philadelphia, and from there caught yet another commuter train up to Hatboro, to visit them.

It was in Upper Darby that one day, near my 16th birthday, I decided to purchase my first guitar. It was a time of folk music topping the popular music charts. As a second grader, my parents had decided that I should learn to play clarinet, and so I did.

I dutifully substituted my school recess time to go to my clarinet lessons. But as a generally hyperactive and sometimes disruptive child, I encountered a substantial roadblock in my budding music career. My third grade teacher, a short, chunky lady named Mrs. G, in her wisdom, decided that whenever I misbehaved, my punishment would be to sit alone in the classroom, instead of attending my clarinet lessons. So my clarinet career faded into the sunset.

In Upper Darby, my plan to finance a guitar with my nearly non-existent income involved my clarinet, still in its tidy, gray case. I knew that there were countless music stores in downtown Philadelphia. As a further cost saving measure, I decided to walk from our home on State Street in Upper Darby, down to 69th Street, and all the way to the heart of Philly. Since the city is a crisscrossed grid of streets assigned names consisting only of numbers, I could observe my progress, numbered intersection by numbered intersection. I walked and walked, clarinet case held in alternating hands. I had no idea how heavy that little case could get.

When I strode into my chosen music store, and stated up front that I had only $25 and a clarinet to exchange for a guitar, the sales person went directly to one specific guitar—a huge, 'f'-hole, country music style guitar. Its glossy, dark sunburst finish covered a hefty plywood construction. Its narrow neck was strung with nearly immovable, bronze-wound steel strings. I had, of course been considering more of a folk-style guitar. I hesitated.

He hauled out a large-format paperback book entitled *The Carcassi Guitar Method*. Then brought out the cheapest, thinnest, cardboard guitar case they carried. Looked like a deal to me.

Back up to 69th Street, I lugged the ponderous guitar, in its case. In my other hand, I carried my new book of guitar method. But I was a gymnast. It would just make me stronger.

I will never forget the whites of my mother's eyes, when I informed her of my new guitar, and the fact that I had traded away my clarinet. I can only imagine what that clarinet cost.

Now that I had put myself on the spot, I spent that entire summer of my 16th year practicing to play guitar at least an hour every single day. I learned to read guitar score, and to play classical guitar compositions, with their complex arpeggios. During the remainder of my free time that summer, I worked at mimicking the lovely fingering styles of folk groups—Peter Paul and Mary, Pete Seeger, and others.

By the time the school year began, I had become a modestly accomplished classical guitarist, as well as a somewhat skilled player—and singer—of many popular folk songs of the day. [Take that, Mrs. G! She was also the teacher who had asserted that the letter 'Q' was always followed by the letter 'U', and backed that up with the offer of a free ice cream cone to any of us who could find a word with a 'Q' that was not followed by a 'U'. I pointed out the world map on the classroom wall. I stood, walked to the map, and placed my finger on Iraq. "That doesn't count, she replied."]

At Upper Darby, I had joined the magnificent High School Chorus, under the inspired direction of Clyde R. Dengler, Jr., and eventually his Concert Choir, in which I blossomed as a lyric tenor. I also joined with a new classmate, Tony, to found a high school gymnastics *club*. This did not become a gymnastics team until the year after I had graduated.

Tony had formal training in Judo, and patiently taught me all the skills he knew. This imparted a sense of confidence in what might have been scary confrontations in later years.

But I tried to progress as a gymnast, on the high bar, the side horse, tumbling (now called "floor exercise") and the long horse (or vaulting horse). I tried every crazy new thing I saw in any televised gymnastics competition. Some of my difficult releases above the high bar were apparently so frightening to watch, that in one instance, Tony, who had been spotting for me, jumped up and caught me around the waist as I was successfully swinging beneath the bar following a release move above the bar and regrasp into a dislocate giant. We both crashed onto the mat. When I told him it was supposed to look like that, we both laughed about it off and on for months.

One fine afternoon, I decided to attempt the hecht vault. Conceptually, it is simple. Spring from the board, reach for the end of the horse with both hands, then launch like a bird, with both arms spread behind and to the side. I didn't understand the physics of it. I launched into the air with both arms spread like a bird, my back fully arched. But then I discovered that I could not rotate my feet toward the mat waiting below. Instead, my entire body tipped forward to a head-down position, with no arms there to cushion the impact. I struck the mat with the top of my head, my body vertical, and crumpled. Dazed, I sat up. When I noticed that others in the gym had gathered in a ring about me, I recall feeling puzzled as to why. Wobbly, I went to the locker room and took a shower. [To this day, my neck CT scan reveals a well-healed, anterior spondylolisthesis of the vertebral body of C3.]

9. Taking a Spin with Janice

1967

I graduated from Upper Darby High School in the spring of 1966, and near that same time, my family once again moved. This time, they moved all the way to St. Louis, Missouri. I enrolled at Eastern Baptist College, still near Philadelphia. I signed up for summer classes, so that I would have a place to live, and in the gap between graduation and the start of those summer classes, I was able to rent a room in the dormitories at Eastern Baptist Seminary. I paid for it by getting a job ($1.25 per hour) as an orderly at Bryn Mawr Hospital.

I spent that summer in introductory college math. When the fall semester started, my only Freshman courses were English Grammar and "Orientation". In high school, I had taken the AP exams for biology and chemistry. Eastern being a small college (about 500 students), I was left with a first semester taking Comparative Histology and Qualitative Analysis with upperclassmen. I joined the College Choir, and became active in their theater productions. I would have made the highest honor roll that first semester, except for receiving a grade of 'D' in "Orientation". I was just not very good at learning about how I was supposed to prepare myself for college learning.

By my second year at Eastern, I had come to know just about every student, instructor and professor there. Many a late night, my roommate, Rich—star pitcher for the baseball team—and I would walk into town (That would be Wayne, Pennsylvania) to have a chicken salad sandwich on toast at the Wayne Diner. A lot of wonderful talking happens between friends walking in the near dark.

One afternoon, while I was pulling out my hair at a sewing machine, attempting to create my complex Archbishop's vestments for our production of Jean Anouilh's *Becket,* Rich wandered into that room off the gymnasium, watched me at the sewing machine for a moment, then said, "Move aside, Rooms. I'll show you a trick." He sat down tugged on the upper thread, tugged at the bobbin thread, then rummaged through the sewing machine's plastic box of feet and bobbins and tiny tools, and extracted a screwdriver.

He instructed me to feel the tension of the needle's thread, compared to the tension of the bobbin's thread. He pointed out that the upper tension setting was as far as it would go. He set that back to neutral, then used the tiny screwdriver to set the bobbin tension to match. The machine performed perfectly. He then confessed that he had worked a summer job as a Singer repairman. Star baseball pitcher and sewing machine pro.

Each Christmas break, I was able to fly to St. Louis and back for $10 each way. The airlines called it a "student discount", but it was a wait at the gate, until the plane was just about to depart. Then they would rake an extra $10 per empty seat, by filling them with impoverished students.

Our College Choir performed locally, several times a year. But over the Easter break each year, we all piled into a bus, and traveled to some distant place. The year before I arrived, they had flown to Haiti, and performed about a dozen concerts there. During my two years at Eastern, our choir traveled through French Canada one Easter break, and through New York state, and into parts of New England the next year.

One of my friends in the College Choir, Janice, was two years ahead of me. She and I enjoyed conversations on those long bus rides during the Easter breaks. She had provided me with valuable tips on how best to get along with "Frosty", the professor of music who ran the choir program, and conducted us at all the concerts. To his face, he was addressed as "Prof."

Frosty was a tall, massive man in his late fifties or early sixties. During the 5 mornings a week, pre-breakfast rehearsals in Eastern's log cabin—an actual hunting lodge visited by Theodore Roosevelt— which was chosen specifically because it was acoustically dead, and would not trick us into thinking we sounded better than we actually did, Frosty would always stand, while we sat and sang. His physical method of conducting the choir was to hold his arms comfortably in front of his barrel chest, hands almost touching, and mark the tempo with the flexion and extension of one index finger. Dynamic expression was signaled by gently rotating both hands, and adjusting the tension of all his fingers. This odd approach forced us to focus on him—on his fingers.

During public performances of the choir, he always wore a solid black robe. To the audience, he was a never moving, black monolith. To add to the mystique of our choir, which sometimes sang unaccompanied by any musical instrument, he added one further slight of hand.

He learned soon after I joined the choir, that I possessed a clear sense of musical pitch. (To this day, I can still usually hum an 'A' whenever I choose, which I always then immediately verify with a pitch pipe I keep in its square, red plastic box in my study.) Frosty gave me a little metal tuning fork, calibrated to 440 'A'. This I was to always keep in a vest pocket beneath my choir robe during performances. I memorized the starting key of each of our *a capella* choral pieces. At the twitch of Frosty's white eyebrow, I would surreptitiously extract the tuning fork, stealthily raise it to my right ear, and then softly hum out the root, third and fifth of the starting key for the next piece. To the audience, which could see no conducting movement, and no clue about the next piece beginning, the effect was startling. I could see it in the body language of those in attendance. Eyes would widen. Faces would turn toward one another. That was how we performed the entirety of Randall Thompson's *The Peaceable Kingdom*.

During one of our Easter bus tours, Janice observed that girls are better at fine sewing crafts, like embroidery, than are boys. That it was an inherent superiority. At our very next stop in a town, I went to the Woolworth's store, and purchased a set of embroidery hoops, specific colors of floss, a pair of white pillow cases, and one needle.

A bookplate that I had used for all of my personal books since starting high school displayed in a woodcut style, a medieval sketch of the Tree of Life rooted into a book. Then and there, on the tour bus, I proceeded to embroider that Tree of Life rooted in a book in four colors on the wide hem of one pillow case. It was about 3" tall and 2½" wide. Green leaves, bright red fruit. Janice shook her head for the remainder of the tour, as I completed it before our return back to campus.

At Christmas of 1967 (my Sophomore year), much of the east coast was blanketed by snow, making travel a challenge. Janice, asked me if I would drive her home to Canton, Ohio in her car. Then I could catch a student flight from the Canton-Akron airport to St. Louis. Not having my own car to drive anywhere made the offer of driving any car an easy one to accept.

The Pennsylvania Turnpike had been fairly well cleared of snow by the time we set out. We started in early evening, and would reach her parents' home near Akron within a few hours. We laughed and chattered and exchanged stories as we zoomed along. Her deep alto laughter resonated somewhere between oboe and bassoon.

My memory of an exact location is fuzzy, but I think it was just after leaving Pennsylvania, and entering Ohio that the roads became intermittently slippery. The roads were nearly empty of other drivers. And there were numerous, temporary construction signs—some blown down, others partly obscured by a veneer of snow. Before I realized that we had somehow missed a road-closed sign, Janice's car spun out. We completely spun around maybe four times, smooth as a skating rink. Her car came to a halt on an incomplete section of highway, about one foot from the end of the concrete pavement, beyond which loomed a precipitous drop. We sat, silent for minutes.

10. Honda 450 Scrambler vs. Semi

1972

This was the end of my second year at the University of Missouri-Columbia School of Medicine. My first year at the school had ended with my wife (and high school sweetheart) and I filing for divorce. The circumstances and suddenness of that left me disoriented.

I had sailed through the first year coursework, and discovered that I was over-educated in the basic sciences. I read every new issue of *Science, Nature*, the *New England Journal of Medicine* and the *Journal of the American Medical Association.* I gobbled up information. While others had struggled, I had shrugged. I decided after one year to pause Medical School classes, and spend my second year in their graduate program, for a Masters Degree in Public Health, specializing in epidemiology, then would rejoin the medical curriculum the in the fall of 1972.

To my astonishment, every graduate class in the Public Health curriculum was easier than most of my undergraduate biology courses. True, there was a lot of content, but after year one of medical school, I found that I could complete all my required reading and assignments in so little time that I was left with nothing much to do, most of the time.

One evening in autumn of 1971, my dear friend, Rob and I sat down in a small bar in downtown Columbia, to sip White Russians, as I recall. He was also taking that year to complete his Masters in Public Health. There, at the piano, a young woman accompanied herself as she convincingly sang a complete set of Carole King's latest albums. And she was beautiful and poised. Her name was Mimi, I learned.

Between sets, I discovered that she was a theater student at Stephens College, also in Columbia—an all girls college. She would be performing a few weeks later in their production of *Fiddler on the Roof*. Her role was that of Tevye's third daughter, Chava, who elopes with a Russian. Who played the men's roles? Mimi said that they had four adult male professional actors/instructors on the staff, and there were a total of six male students on full scholarships, to earn their degree in fine arts.

I later discovered that one of their past professional actors was George C. Scott, of *Patton* fame. Several of their current professional male actors later went on to minor roles in several Hollywood films.

"I'm going to that play," I stated to Rob, as we left the bar. "Want to come?"

"I think you should go alone. Do you have a decent suit?"

The following day, Rob gave me a beautiful blue pinstripe suit that had been passed on to him by his uncle, but that Rob could not wear, since his own arms were too long for the sleeves. The sleeves were too long for my arms, so I dropped it off at a tailor's shop in Columbia for adjustments.

The opening night of *Fiddler*, I dressed in my new old suit, and went to the playhouse, to watch Mimi. Having been deeply involved in theater productions myself, I always enjoy a live performance. This time was no different. After the curtain fell, I asked my way to the dressing room, which can allow a dozen or more actors to sit before one of the ranks of well-lit wall mirrors lining two of its walls, and apply their makeup. The private dressing areas were elsewhere.

On entering the makeup room, I immediately spotted Mimi, and just watched from a distance for a bit, as she began to remove her stage makeup. Her friend, Paula, who had also been at the piano in the bar where I first met Mimi, saw me standing there, and whispered to Mimi. When Mimi turned around, her face seemed to light up. We spoke for a bit, with the conversation ending with my asking her out to dinner later that week. She accepted.

Stephens College had its own, stand-alone, vintage playhouse. There is something magical—perhaps mystical—about the assemblage of dressing rooms, back-stage areas, teasers and tormentors [backdrop and side curtains that block the audience's view of the stage walls behind the proscenium curtain], the countless ropes and pulleys, and especially the well-worn stage floor, often with residual scraps of tape and marks—fading artifacts of the blocking for previous shows.

Dating Mimi over the following months was a mixture of joy at her vivacity, and simultaneously sobering. When a portion of their theater troupe traveled over the Christmas break from Columbia, Missouri to Michigan City, Indiana, to perform at a playhouse, I followed them there in my car—a slant-6 powered, 1960 Dodge Dart, that my brother had given me, after my first new car, a 1969 Chevy Nova, went away in my uncontested divorce settlement. Don McLean's *American Pie* was at the top of the pop charts, and played nearly non-stop on the radio for that entire trip.

Mimi asked if I would drive her from Michigan City to her home in Bonner Springs, Kansas. Of course, yes! It lay just west of Kansas City, so we stopped at my mother's house in St. Louis along the way.

She appeared to be delighted to meet Mimi. But her eyes widened, when our home phone rang, and Mimi immediately answered it.

"Hi. This is Mimi."

Mimi's home turned out to be a rather substantial mansion within an exclusive, gated community. It was late, so I spent the night there. By the following day, I had noticed that Mimi's vivacity had toned itself down to a meekness that I had never seen before. [I would later discover that nearly every girl in the theater department at Stephens College had a prescription for one weight-loss drug or another. These were typically dexadrine or methadrine, or even biphetamine. Most of them were not at all overweight, but they used the prescriptions to increase their "energy" for acting. When they did not take it, such as during visits home, their personalities returned to reality, as did Mimi's on this occasion.]

The following morning, my Dodge Dart refused to start, and had to be towed to a nearby repair shop to have the starter replaced. So I spent an additional, unplanned day at Mimi's house. I felt not as welcomed as on the first day.

During that wild "Public Health Masters" year, I performed on-stage in two different theater productions at Stephens College. I played 5-string banjo for Richardson & Birney's, *Dark of the Moon*, and was cast in a lead role in the Newley & Bricusse musical, *Roar of the Greasepaint, Smell of the Crowd*. During the production run of the latter, both my mother and my medical school's Assistant Dean attended. And there I was, in white-face clown makeup, with a painted-on teardrop below my eye, singing and speaking in a heavy, Cockney accent. *"Who can I turn to when nobody needs me? My heart wants to know, and so I must go where destiny leads me. With no star to guide me, and no one beside me, I'll go on my way, and after the day the darkness will hide me."*

I was offered a full, Fine Arts scholarship to attend Stephens College. Soon thereafter, the University of Missouri Graduate Department of Fine Arts offered me a full scholarship in Theater. I reluctantly turned them both down.

Mimi and I seemed to enjoy each other's company—until I decided that I would, indeed, return to medical school, to complete my MD degree. Our relationship then fizzled out.

Early that summer, I purchased a used, bright red Honda 450 Scrambler motorcycle, which was an underweight, overpowered off-road bike (with only a 1-hour gas tank) that I used for street transportation. Never mind the knobby tires and harsh suspension. I added two chrome side-bars, to protect my knees, and a chrome luggage rack behind its 2-person, banana seat.

I traveled on it from Columbia, Missouri to Chaptico, Maryland, to visit Richard and Diane. I departed Columbia at night.

In the wee hours, cruising at 70 mph just south of a city (I cannot recall what city), I passed left of a slowly moving semi, with its caution lights blinking. I thought little of it. The Interstate loop there was three lanes across. I was in the leftmost lane. Then I saw why the lights were blinking. Across all three lanes, another semi had come to a halt sideways. Its reverse lights came on, as it backed further into my lane. I moved to the left shoulder, and passed it at 70 mph with 4" to spare between the rear bumper of the backing semi to my right, and the left guardrail to my left.

11. Honda 450 Scrambler vs. Coal Truck

1972

Kathy, another acting student at Stephens College lived in Middlesboro, Kentucky. On this same trip to Chaptico, I had arranged to visit her, and spend the night at their house. I arrived in mid-morning, having driven through half of Missouri and nearly all of Kentucky during the night.

Kathy was mildly pleased to see me. Her father, whose source of employment I don't recall, was thrilled to see—my Honda 450 Scrambler. He urged me to take him for a ride on it, in back of me. I agreed, despite Kathy's eye roll at the thought.

As we rode about, he eventually directed me to a well tucked-away, fenced-in building, labeled, "American Legion Club—Members Only." The gravel parking lot inside the unlocked gate was nearly half-full of tattered vehicles at mid-morning. We waited outside the solid door, while we were scrutinized by an eyeball looking through a tiny peep hole lens.

The door buzzed, and we went inside. The American Legion Club there appeared to be a large, single room that was essentially a liquor bar. This was a "speak-easy" in a dry county. I politely sipped a beer while Kathy's dad expounded to his friends about his incredible ride on the Honda 450 Scrambler. He opened the solid door and gestured. About a dozen of them stepped into the open doorway to have a brief look, then returned to their assorted ethanol beverages.

From what I could gather, this group of fellow drinkers constituted an economically depressed segment of the Middlesboro population. They gathered here daily to commiserate over their employment woes.

That evening, Kathy and I rode up to a beautiful area of the mountain foothills, and enjoyed the sunset. When we returned to her house, I begged my leave, and went to bed. I had been awake for nearly 36 hours at that point.

I departed early in the morning, and headed for the Cumberland Gap, in the corner of far-southwest Virginia. The winding, unmarked blacktop highway through the mountains was a motorcyclist's scenic dream. I could, on the other hand, see why the early pioneers, driving their mule-drawn, ox-drawn and horse-drawn, Conestoga wagons westward were overjoyed to have finally gotten clear of that same road—all dirt and mud back then—as they entered Kentucky.

But I was heading the opposite direction, and driving a Honda 450 Scrambler. The morning was cloudless, so far as I could see through breaks in the nearly constant tree coverage of the road. The frequent, sharp curves of the road allowed me to lean my bike at breathtaking angles—first to one side, then the other. Never mind that there was no shoulder at all. And no guardrail. Only massive, oaks and hickory trees encroaching on the crumbling edge of the asphalt.

At one sharp, ascending curve to the left—forever imprinted into my memory, I was mid-curve, leaning so low to the pavement that my left side-bar was nearly touching. The right side of the pavement tipped away downward to my right. A coal truck came suddenly into view, descending rapidly, while riding over the center of the road. On seeing me, the driver applied his brakes. The contents of the coal truck bed were not covered—only a mounding pile of coal. Several pounds of coal spilled out over the lane in front of me.

My Honda's knobby tires began to skip over the coal, allowing the bike to drift rapidly toward the right pavement edge and its awaiting tree trunks. With only a couple of inches of pavement remaining, I cruised beyond the scattered chunks of coal, and climbed easily up the remainder of the steep curve.

12. Honda 450 Scrambler Tailgating in the Rain

1972

During my return ride from Chaptico, Maryland, to Columbia, Missouri, after having visited with Richard and Diane, my motorcycle drive chain slowly disintegrated. I kept oiling it by hand, and adjusting the screws to take up the slack, and just barely arrived home before it gave out completely.

That was the good news. Also during that return ride, my air-cooled, 450 cc engine seemed to be overheating and burning oil. As the filthy, dark cloud of combusted oil belched out the dual exhaust pipes, I stopped frequently to add more oil to the crank case. The engine steadily lost power, limping into my driveway in Columbia with a battered drive chain and cooked engine.

I rented a trailer, and drove the dead motorcycle to a repair shop south of Columbia. "Make it happy again."

By now, I had become involved in a serious relationship with Rita, a University of Missouri undergraduate who was 4 years my junior. She was well known in Columbia as an active feminist. She even wrote a column in an "underground" newspaper, published weekly. Rita proudly refused to shave her armpits.

As the summer was drawing to a close, with my medical school classes scheduled to resume within a few weeks, I suggested that she and I ride the Honda 450 Scrambler to visit Richard and Diane in Chaptico, as soon as the bike had been repaired. She agreed enthusiastically.

Rita drove me down to the repair shop, and dropped me off. The owner explained that I had burned up the pistons. He had saved one of them to show me. It was about the diameter of a can of baked beans, and half as tall. Embedded into the once-molten metal of the piston's upper surface, little fragments of shattered piston rings were entrapped like fossils.

"Can I have that?" I asked.

"Sure."

"I think it would make a nice ashtray."

He frowned. "I don't think it can take any more heat."

The following morning, Rita and I set out for Chaptico. She sandwiched herself between me and the large duffle bag that I had strapped to my chrome luggage rack above the rear wheel. I had also added fold-down foot pegs for her.

The morning went wonderfully, but by late afternoon, it had begun to rain. We stopped, and improvised some rain gear from our belongings. Rita hopped back on, with a rain poncho tied about her torso with string. Within minutes of resuming the trip, both of us were completely soaked, and agreed to just continue, since the late August weather was warm.

What I had not anticipated was that as the increasingly heavy rain began to pool on the surface of the Interstate highway, my knobby tires would lose traction. I could sense in the handlebars the fading resistance to turning. This became a particular danger when we passed semi trucks, with their front shock wave of wind attempting to shove me away from the passing lane, and into the median strip.

I decided to just follow one of them, and never pass. At the abruptly square rear of a moving semi, there is another wind issue, from aerodynamic drag, generating buffeting winds.

An additional problem was that the previously heavy rain had become torrential—the kind that might cause the driver of an automobile to just pull off the highway, and wait out the worst of it.

The only path along the pavement that was relatively clear of water pooling was right in the tracks of the semi's rear tires, to either side of the trailer's center line. And the only distance that avoided the worst of the drag buffeting so close to the side was about 10 to 15 feet behind the trailer's rear bumper.

So we zoomed along at 75-80 mph, 10 to 15 feet behind the semi.

13. Going for a Dip in The Surf at Puerta Vallarta

1977

A lot happens over five years. I sold my Honda 450 Scrambler after one year. Rita and I lived together for several years, then we formally married. After my final year of medical school, when I began a Pediatrics intership at the Missouri Medical Center, we rented an old farmhouse that sat on 100 acres of farmland in the steep river hills just north of the Missouri River, near Ashland, Missouri. The rental came with mature fruit orchards, a large garden with a productive asparagus patch, and two horses—a barrel racer and a quarter horse—a barn full of horse tack, and permission to ride them whenever we liked, in exchange for tossing them some hay during the winter.

Rita was enrolled as a graduate student in the Master of Social Work (MSW) program, also at Missou. But we hardly saw one another. I was on duty for in-house call every third night. I would go in one morning at 6 am, work all day, work wide-awake all that night, then work all day the second day, before returning home. After each 36 hour stretch, I would arrive home an exhausted zombie. I would work a normal 12-hour work day the third day, and come home a somewhat normal person, then start the cycle again the following morning.

Some of my night shifts included filling out death certificates for two or more tiny, premature babies. I signed more death certificates during my first six months as an intern than I did in total for the remainder of my medical career.

Late in the Autumn, Rita moved out. She was unable to clearly explain why, but in retrospect, it should have come as no surprise to me. We had gone from happily sharing our lives to hardly sharing anything. All the while, Rita came home to an isolated farmhouse, far from her friends.

I fell apart, exhausted and befuddled. Two marriages—poof! My daily performance at the hospital faltered, with the Chairman of Pediatrics insisting that I take a few weeks off. I agreed. I went home to the deserted, isolated farmhouse, with an atypically harsh winter dropping feet of snow. There I sat for days, occasionally braving the bitter cold and winds to split some of the dead hickory logs that I had cut during better times. When the logs had all been converted into heat for the drafty house, I ended up fueling the wood stove with the copious notes that I had laboriously written during my five years as a medical and graduate student—thousands of pages.

My former classmate, Rob, now lived in San Francisco, and discovered that Mt. Zion Hospital was searching for one additional Pediatrics intern, to start in January of 1976. I jumped at the chance to go anywhere else. I boxed up all my books, and hauled them to the Ashland Post Office, and mailed 17 cartons (70 pounds each) to Rob. I flew to San Francisco with a footlocker as baggage.

I had been something of a thorn in the side of the Pediatrics Department at Missou. Once, when the nursery had so many babies that they ran out of bassinets in which to place them, they improvised by purchasing a dozen Rubbermaid totes, placing them onto empty carts. The Missouri legislature was balking at fully funding the Medical Center's budget. With the thought of prompting public outcry at the legislature, I phoned the local TV station, and told them the bassinet situation and remedy. A TV crew appeared in the hospital within an hour, explaining what Dr. Goff had told them. The Pediatrics Chairman was not pleased. It went on the evening news. The entire medical faculty was irate. I tended to rock boats.

When I arrived at Mt. Zion Hospital, to keep my first appointment with Dr. Roberta Ballard, I detailed my recent events, and readily confessed to having been a pain in the ass at Missou. At my followup interview, she said that she had called and spoken with my previous boss, who confirmed everything I had said, including that I was a pain in the ass. "How soon can you start?"

As soon as my first paycheck arrived, I moved out of Rob's Victorian house on Pine Street, and into an apartment a block away, on California. With Rob's assistance, I purchased a battered Ford Galaxy from one of his old friends. When my cartons of books arrived, 3 were completely lost, two more were substantially damaged, and one of them contained a stack of Spanish language school books on sex education. [The US Post Office had recently installed a new, automated package handling system.] Gone were my Latin American Literature books, all of my math books, and about a dozen dearly purchased medical textbooks.

Some evenings and into the night, I would walk alone, up and down the streets of San Francisco. In areas of the city where the traffic was light, but the neighborhood looked worrisome, I would actually walk down the center of the street. All the while, I ruminated on my two failed marriages before my 28th birthday, my loss of a compass foot to navigate my life. I learned the layout of the city first hand: streets to the docks, to the tourist traps, up and down absurdly steep grades. I would occasionally ride a cable car into the city's heart, explore a bit, then walk back home in the light of street lamps.

I eventually felt revitalized. Soon, I met Elizabeth, a divorced mother of two middle-schoolers, who was a Respiratory Therapy student at Mt. Zion Hospital. She had finished her coursework, and was doing her "intership" at the Mt. Zion intensive care nursery (ICN). Slight of build, she scarcely reached 5 feet in height. We began to date.

Her home was not in San Francisco. She lived in a 1903 vintage, brown shingle house in a quiet neighborhood of Berkeley, California. On occasion, I would sit at the antique, square grand piano in her living room, and sing some of the songs I had performed in the musical productions at Stephens College, accompanying myself at the keyboard. I purchased a set of piano-tuning tools, and tuned the piano.

After living in San Francisco for a half-year, walking back and forth to work at the hospital, and driving across the Bay Bridge to visit with Elizabeth, I moved into her house in Berkeley. Then my commute became a traffic-plagued drive across the Bay Bridge, morning and evening.

We married early that autumn, in a low-key, ceremony in the home of one of her friends. I didn't even tell my mother about it, until after it was a *fait accompli*. I planted a vegetable garden in the back yard, with my first attempt at "deeply-dug," high yield growing. I pruned the aging fruit trees, and cut away massive, towering vines that had, over the decades, overgrown the tops of the trees. So we had fresh plums and loquats, which had previously just been ignored. We made jams and jellies.

From time to time, the four of us would go out to eat at the many fancy restaurants in the Bay Area. Together, we drove into San Francisco to watch the first run of Star Wars.

In the spring of 1977, we flew down to the stunning beach city of Puerta Vallarta, along the Pacific coast of Mexico. The four of us went to the best restaurants, and listened to the Mariachi bands. There was the usual stormy weather just off the coast. We took tourist boat trips, and endlessly browsed the markets, on one occasion purchasing a whole kilo of raw prawns to cook back at the beach villa we had rented for the week. (The cost was stunningly low, due to political "unrest" that was plaguing the Jalisco state at the time. Police were visible everywhere.)

On the first day that the surf had calmed enough to consider going into the water, we walked down to the beach in our bathing suits. It looked wonderful, despite the occasionally choppy waves. I waded out, only about 6 feet from the sandy beach, and immediately discovered that its precipitous slope beyond the beach meant that I could not stand with my head above the water.

A wave crested over me. It did not drag me farther out. Instead, it tumbled in a ferociously tight swirl parallel to the shore, and held me in its grip. I found that I was unable to surface for air, and at the same time, was unable to touch the sand beneath me. I could not breathe, and could not escape. As the air in my lungs diminished, and my oxygen-starved body and mind lapsed into hopelessness, the water, with no effort on my part, spat me out onto the damp sand of the beach.

14. Best in USAFE—Ramstein

1982

Back in Berkeley, I had finished my Pediatrics residency, including a fellowship in Neonatology at Oakland Children's Hospital. I had applied and been accepted into the graduate program at U.C. Berkeley School of Public Health to work toward a Doctorate of Public Health in the field of Maternal and Child Health. They would grant me a full scholarship, as well as a stipend of $500 each month.

I had purchased my very first computer in 1977, a SOL-20 "microcomputer", complete with an 8080a processor and a full 48K of RAM memory. I equipped it with three 5¼" floppy disc drives (there were no hard drives yet), an 8" floppy drive and a floor-model DEC dot-matrix printer—30 characters per second!

With my medical school friend, Roger, I founded Berkeley Medical Data Associates, and began to write and sell software for medical applications. At this time in my life, my hair reached down to my shoulders, and my full beard to mid-chest.

Elizabeth had envisioned herself married to a wealthy physician, rather than an underpaid, itinerant Public Health expert. Even the prospect of a long-term appointment to a university faculty did not meet with her approval. I placed my career plan of many years against my history of two previously failed marriages. The choices were agonizing.

When my youngest brother, Jon, came out to visit, he expressed interest in joining the US Air Force. I arranged to accompany him to a recruiter. The recruiter tidily snagged Jon. Once this astute recruiter, a Master Sergeant, learned that I was a fully trained physician, he made his pitch to me: start off with a long-term assignment in Europe, with free moving expenses and transportation there and back for my entire family; subsequent possible deployment to Japan or the Philippines; go in as a Captain.

Jon enlisted. I went home and discussed my offer with Elizabeth and the kids. The thought of living and traveling in Europe, with the prospect of further world travel, met universal approval. I signed-up to go in.

One day, I went home, and shaved off my entire beard and mustache, then immediately went to a barber in Oakland. "A regulation military hair cut, please."

"Are you sure about that?"

When I returned home that afternoon, Elizabeth and the kids saw my head and face for the very first time—after more than three years. For the next couple of weeks, whenever any of them would look at me, they would struggle to control their spontaneous laughter.

A glitch. My expected assignment in Germany "fell through." But if I spent a year at Tyndall AFB, in the Florida panhandle, then I would be assured an assignment to Ramstein AB the following year.

Off to Tyndall we went. I will spare my readers the saga of living, if only for a year, in what was known locally as "South Alabama". Our house had a backyard pool, and the white sand beaches of Panama City (and of Tyndall AFB itself) were a delight.

The following summer, we were flown across the Atlantic Ocean—with our young son, Micah, only two and a half. Our newly rented, roomy, two story house in the charming town of Ramstein was situated several miles off the air base.

The two older kids were enrolled in the schools on base, while Micah was enrolled in a pre-school within the small, German town. They spoke only German there. We worried that Micah might find it overly stressful to be placed in a non-English speaking setting, with both the teachers and his fellow classmates speaking only a language he did not understand. My own knowledge of German was of marginal, tourist quality.

I took him there his first morning. A gray-haired frau came out to their lobby to greet us. Then she spoke directly to Micah, in German, with a charm and grandmotherly vivacity that, to my amazement, caused him to voluntary take her hand, and follow her into the bowels of the preschool. Just before he vanish, his 2½ year old face turned to me with a smile, and he waved goodbye.

On the base, I served as Chief of Pediatrics at the Ramstein Clinic, a department that included two talented nurse practitioners, both Majors and Viet Nam War veterans, as well as another Pediatrician, also a Captain. (His date of rank was a smidgen later than my date of rank. In a clinic, Doctor trumps nurse practitioner.)

Nearly every town and village in Germany at that time offered its own volksmarch annually, with several nearby to choose from every weekend. They were well-marked routes through forests and fields and village streets, starting and ending at the high school's gymnasium. Typically, they offered a choice of either a 10k or 20k walk on a Saturday or Sunday morning. (I always selected the 10k.) It was never timed. There was no first or last noted. At its completion, each participant was awarded a distinctive souvenir of the occasion—sometimes a custom medal suspended on a short or long ribbon, sometimes a souvenir metal or ceramic plate.

On most volksmarches, I brought Micah along, allowing him to walk alongside me for as much of it as he wished, then would lift him onto my shoulders for the remainder. Sometimes his sister would also join us. I can say that seeing a country—a culture—on foot is the finest and most intimate mode of travel.

Ramstein Air Base is a huge place, with a substantial population of US and NATO-member personnel and aircraft: fighter squadrons, transport squadrons, strategic squadrons, and helicopter squadrons. To keep it all safe, from crime and the occasional terrorist threat (usually domestic), there was also a large number of USAF Military Police. They manned its entry gates and secure areas, and patrolled the streets and roads of the base. They were the folks who, upon seeing the small, "officer" sticker on my driver-side front bumper when I approached the security booth at any of the gates, would snap to attention, and salute me.

Each year, the USAFE (US Air Force in Europe) headquarters people would review performance records from all the US Air Force military police units throughout all its bases in European countries.

Then they would select one unit to be the "Best in USAFE" for that year. The winning unit would get a ribbon to add to their uniform insignia.

In 1982, part-way through my second year at Ramstein, our very own security police were awarded "Best in USAFE." They celebrated that evening, and into the night at one of the clubs on base.

The following morning, I hopped into my 1977 Dodge Aspen station wagon (shipped from Florida to Ramstein by the AF for free), and headed out of the village of Ramstein, toward Ramstein AB. At a left hand turn where the road from the village met the main road on the air base, only about 100 yards from the security checkpoint, I stopped behind two other cars headed in the same direction, and waited for a break in the base traffic to allow them to make the turn.

A Security Police cruiser zoomed out of the base, not even slowing at the guard booth, then turned at high-speed onto my road. It was clearly out of control. It missed the first two cars waiting at the stop sign, and missed the front half of my Aspen wagon. With surprising force, it slammed at an angle into the driver-side of my car, just a couple of inches behind my seat, spinning my car partially around, and in the process, crushing in my left passenger door and rear seat. I was uninjured.

Best in USAFE. In 1982, obtaining car body parts to repair a five year old American car required over a month to arrive, then another couple of weeks for the repairs to be completed.

On a happier note, the base bowling alley snack bar served the finest beef hot dogs on the planet: a juicy rindworst with a firm skin that popped when you bit into it. I ate lunch there every working day.

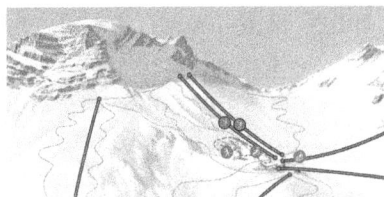

15. The Zugspitze White-Out

1983

During that winter, shortly after Micah had turned five, he and I traveled to Garmisch-Partenkirschen, a German ski resort in southern Bavaria, up against their southern border with Austria. The boundary there, following a high ridge of the Alps, includes Germany's highest mountain peak, the Zugspitze.

We stayed at the Edelweiss Inn, which is a huge winter resort facility operated by the US military. Since I was then on active duty, the cost for a week was a pittance. They even offered ski classes for kids.

Each evening, I would ask him where he would like to eat. The town itself is host to numerous wonderful restaurants with cuisine from all over Europe. I would make suggestions. But Micah always chose the McDonald's, and would always order the Quarter Pounder. By the end of the week I realized that his choice was determined solely by the fact that he wanted to collect the hinged, Styrofoam boxes in which the Quarter Pounder was sold.

I enrolled him in a ski class for children, but he was unhappy with it. So I would, instead, take him to the bunny slopes myself, and instruct him in the basics, such as snowplowing and simple turns. After frequently staring at the assorted transports and lifts heading up the mountain, I decided that we should go up higher.

We rode a cogwheel train, with stair-stepped cars, up to the highest lodge. We wore our rented ski boots, and carried our rented skis with us. In addition to rooms there, which we would not be renting, there were a number of dining locations within the multi-story lodge. We ate and shopped for souvenirs.

Shortly after lunch, I followed signs to ski trails. Snow had been falling heavily all day. The ski trail signs often showed a difficulty symbol, such as a blue square or diamond, or for the most difficult trails, a black diamond or double black diamond. I looked out at the huge, snow-filled bowl that extended from the very top of the mountain ridge down to much lower on the mountain.

An interesting trail sign showed no visible difficulty rating, and seemed to head in a direction that would gently traverse the upper bowl at nearly no downward slope. The heavy snow continued. Below, in the distance, I could barely visualize a number of ski lifts that returned back to the highest lodge. The trail seemed perfect.

On our skis, I kept Micah between my legs, and supported him beneath his arms, as he snowplowed his way along. But the side slope became progressively steeper, requiring me to labor quite a bit to keep our forward motion traversing that relatively level course of what I believed to be the trail intended by the sign I had followed.

After about 20 minutes of laborious traverse, we were skiing in a total white-out. I could see nothing above or below me, and could mostly sense slope by its feel on my skis. I decided to give up on the hypothetical trail, and just head downward into the lower part of the bowl.

Together, we slowly zigzagged our way downward. Through the densely falling snow, I saw that we had passed the origin of one of the lifts that returned to the upper lodge. In a wild guess, I steered toward a random sideways direction, hoping to eventually see the remaining lift. My eyes ached from straining to see anything through the bright white snow above me, below me and in front of me.

We finally found that last lift to the high lodge, and rode it back to where we would be able to catch the cogwheel train back down the mountain. I was exhausted, and feeling foolish. To try to figure out where we had skied, I returned to the location of those trail signs, now caked with even more snow. With a brush of my glove, the sign we had followed revealed a double black diamond: advanced experts only.

The following day, I realized that we had come precariously close to going over the ridge, into Austria, and more frightening, that the bowl ends at an 800 foot pour-off, below the lift that we had taken.

An F-15b "Tub" at Eglin AFB

16. Machine Gun at My Heart: Port Sudan

1983

In the fall of 1981, I traveled to Brooks Air Force Base, outside San Antonio, Texas, for a six week course in Aerospace Medicine, to train as a flight surgeon—a step that would improve my opportunities for promotion within the Medical Corps.

On my return, I was placed on flying status, which meant that I was required to log an average of 1 hour of flying time each week. With my newly pinned wings, and newly issued flight suits, I would ride along on transports, helicopter training missions, and medical evacuation journeys. Sometimes these flights were local to the region of Ramstein, while others ventured to Munich, Amsterdam and as far away as the Atlantic coast of southern Spain. There was no tourism involved, but simply fulfillment of whatever duties were assigned to each particular flight or exercise. I would always carry a military-issued passport, as well as my NATO medical ID card, identifying me as a "non-combatant."

These nearly weekly flights would often consume an entire morning or afternoon, or even an entire day. And the total flight time accumulated toward my average of 50 flight hours per year. The remainder of my duty time was spent in the Ramstein Clinic or serving in local readiness exercises.

I was also paired with the base Veterinarian to regularly perform health inspections of the food and sanitary facilities throughout the base. That included deciding which incidental animal bites and other unusual animal exposures would require that a service member or dependent initial anti-rabies prophylaxis (shots).

All of my varied activities made for what I considered to be a remarkably enjoyable career path. I also held a high regard for our single-payer health care system. Finances and health insurance were never a consideration in providing health care to every active duty service member or their dependents. All my medical decisions were founded on medical need.

By the summer of 1983, I had been promoted to the rank of Major, completed my tour at Ramstein, and my third marriage had ended. I moved alone to my next assignment at Eglin Air Force Base, which is on Florida's panhandle coast between Tyndall AFB and the city of Pensacola. My stepson had graduated from High School in Ramstein, at the age of 16, and had gone off to MIT to study engineering. At the same time, Elizabeth moved with Micah and my stepdaughter to Tucson, Arizona.

At Eglin, I was no longer a pediatrician. I served as the senior flight surgeon for the 33rd Tactical Fighter Wing, and directly as the flight surgeon for the 58th Tactical Fighter Squadron—which flew the new F-15 fighter aircraft. I, of course, always sat in the second seat of the F-15B, while all the other F-15A aircraft had only a single seat. The "B" was lovingly referred to as "the Tub" by the pilots. Later models of the F-15 eventually all had two seats, when the F-15 transitioned from being a premier, high-altitude air-superiority fighter to being used more for air-to-ground weapon attacks. That back seat then became the routine seat for the weapons officer.

Shortly after arriving at Eglin, I learned that I and my three enlisted medics would be sent for a two month assignment in the late fall to Riyadh, Saudi Arabia. I read all that I could find about the history and current situation in the Arabian Peninsula.

This was a strange window of time, during which the US directly supported Saddam Housain's war with Iran. One of our military contributions was to maintain an AWACS radar aircraft always observing and reporting aircraft movements throughout the region. This was carried out round the clock, and required three of the radar aircraft, all their on-board staffing, all the aircraft maintenance staffing, ground radar crews, and all manner of support personnel, altogether comprising a deployment of about 400 people.

The deployment reached the numerical threshold of requiring a clinic with a physician, a chaplain, food services, security forces, logistics and lodging coordinators, etc. Three aircraft: 400 people.

My clearest image of Saudi Arabia is a place with no green. Only dull yellow and rusty red sand. No grass, no trees, no hazy blue mountain ridges off in the distance. Just hot, windy sand. The exception was Riyadh itself, where there were scores of towering, construction cranes, raising one new skyscraper or high-rise after another. Oil money. Every manner of artifice was actively employed to obscure the reality that most of the Arabian peninsula is only marginally inhabitable, at best.

There was mystique. And the souks were remarkable—fabric souks, rug souks, brass-ware souks. Curiously, nothing of any interest or value sold in the souks was made in Saudi Arabia, which is a purely consumer culture, living off the rich profits of oil extraction (also performed by foreigners).

While I was deployed there, I ran our small clinic, conducted food service inspections, and measured electromagnetic radiation from microwave ovens as well as from ground radar and communications equipment. My one 12-hour flight aboard an E3A, circling high above eastern Arabia, logged two months of required flight time.

Shortly before I was scheduled to return to Florida, I was informed that the US Air Force needed to hire a civilian physician who was currently resident in Sudan. There was a small number of Air Force members stationed at a logistics base there, and needed a source of medical care. They needed for me to travel there, review his medical credentials, and officially decide if he was qualified.

I inquired if I could bring one of my enlisted medics with me, to assist with the process and record keeping. They approved it. In reality, I did not feel comfortable traveling into Sudan alone.

The two of us flew from Riyadh to Jiddah, on the Red Sea Coast. For the layover day that we were there, we visited the American Consulate, then became tourists in civilian clothing, roaming the ancient city.

Our flight to Port Sudan was aboard a Sudan Airways jumbo jet. As we boarded, I noticed that for the width of the fuselage, one-third of its total seating, all at the rear, was piled nearly to the cabin roof with luggage, boxes and obvious souvenirs from the Pilgrimage. The remaining two thirds of the cabin was completely jammed with passengers, most with additional carry-on items in their laps. I assumed the baggage holds were also filled to capacity. This was a clearly (intentionally) overloaded aircraft. My medic and I looked at one another and grimaced.

As we completed taxiing, and accelerated for lift-off, the huge aircraft rotated, tail section down, but remained with its rear wheels on the runway until maybe two dozen yards of the runway remained. Finally, with engines screaming, it took to the air. Yikes!

When we made final approach to the airport in Port Sudan, I immediately spotted a derelict C-3 transport plane resting to the side of the runway, half-way down its modest length. It had an eight-foot diameter hole in the right side of its fuselage. Our landing was uneventful. [I later learned that a huge, electrical generator had been placed on an unanchored pallet aboard the C-3. It was left unsecured with the approval of the airline, because "it was too heavy to move on its own". As soon as that plane had rotated on takeoff, the generator and its pallet had slid directly through the side of the fuselage. Oops.]

The airport terminal was guarded by Sudanese soldiers, each carrying an automatic, assault weapon. All of the soldiers were quite tall, and remarkably gaunt. Their eyes appeared bloodshot, and darted rapidly from one passenger to another. As we approached the customs gate, the soldier there widened his eyes at the two of us—the only white people to have disembarked, among the mass of likely native Sudanese passengers.

He asked me several incomprehensible, brief questions, all the while pointing the barrel of his weapon directly at my heart, a mere one foot away. With a broad smile, I slowly explained in English, supplemented by the few applicable words of Arabic that I had learned, that my medic and I were Americans, and that we we coming to speak with a doctor in town.

I doubt that he understood what I was saying. With an irritated expression, he dismissively waved us out the door with his free hand.

17. F-15 at 50,000 Feet

1984

Our trip to Port Sudan was a waste of time, in my mind. We drove out into a bleak, sandy plain to visit the doctor, located in a 20-foot trailer that served as both his clinic and his home. His credentials were impeccable. As it turned out, he was a fully board certified physician working for *Médecins Sans Frontières*, or Doctors Without Borders, a highly respected organization that provides medical care throughout the world.

Our return journey from Port Sudan, also on Sudan Airways, felt safer from an aeronautical standpoint. But during the flight between Port Sudan and Khartoum, the stewardess served us a chunk of bread from a basket, along with an unpackaged chunk of mystery cheese. This was washed down with water from a large pitcher. I've never been particularly squeamish, but I had studied enough parasitology to have some concern.

In Khartoum, we eventually transferred to another flight. But while we sat on the front steps of the airport, a loaded cattle truck pulled into the circle in front of us. We looked at one another, then both said, simultaneously, "They wouldn't." They didn't. We flew to Cairo, then on to Turkey, with an overnight between flights. That free time resulted in my purchasing 8 or 9 carved meerschaum tobacco pipes for myself, most of which I still have as I write this.

During another holdover, this time in Britain, prior to flying back across the Atlantic, and returning to Eglin, I snagged a tweed sports coat, which still fits me at the age of 74.

What fighter pilots do, when they are not fighting in a war is practice, practice, practice. Most of our training missions were flown over the southeastern US. Occasionally one or more of our three squadrons of F-15s would deploy to another air force base, or Air National Guard base at some distance from Florida.

On one training deployment, we traveled to Nellis Air Force Base, near Las Vegas, Nevada. This was a "Red Flag" exercise, with aircraft squadrons from multiple branches of the US military. The flight from Eglin to Nellis is a long one, and we flew it at relatively high altitude (over 40,000 feet), in bright, clear skies. We flew in wide formations of 4 aircraft, often a mile or more apart.

As we were crossing New Mexico, the pilot of my aircraft needed to perform some navigational calculations related to our final way points to Nellis. We were the last plane in a 4-flight, with the closest perhaps two miles from us. He asked me to keep us on course for a few minutes. We were on autopilot, but that sometimes requires small corrections.

I am not a pilot, though I have unofficially been at the controls in rare moments. After we had been soaring along in a straight line for a while, I noticed that we were slowly drifting closer to our neighbor ahead and to the right. I gave it a bit of rudder, and left stick, at which our aircraft obediently rolled its wings slightly, along with a slight left yaw.

The size of our neighbor gradually increased. I repeated the control movements more aggressively. Again, once we had righted, we were still approaching our neighbor at the same apparent rate. Finally, I grabbed the attention of the pilot via our intercom.

"Shit!"

The afterburner kicked in. He rolled us so suddenly to the left that my helmet banged against the right side of the canopy. We violently pulled downward and away from our neighbor, righted, then assumed a more suitable position as his wingman.

"I hope nobody saw that, Doc." After a pause, he explained that at such a high altitude, control surfaces have very little air to work against. In retrospect, we were probably 10 to 15 seconds from a mid-air collision, had he not taken the controls when he did.

18. F-15 Furball over Nevada

1984

The ramp (the name given to the parking area of active aircraft at an air base or airport) at Nellis was something to behold. Every aircraft from each branch of service which would participate during the Red Flag exercise was spread from one end to the other. Scores of them, each with their distinctive airframe design, and proudly marked with their unit insignia and home "base."

In simple terms, there were surveillance aircraft, bristling with antennae, assault aircraft, and assorted models of fighters galore— some with a single jet engine, others with two. F-16s appeared like gnats alongside the F-15s. Prior to one of my flights, I climbed up the ladder, and onto the wing root of my F-15b—the "tub", the two-seat model that none of the F-15 pilots really wanted to be stuck having to fly. I paused for a long while, surveying the spectacular scene. Then stooped beneath the canopy, and climbed into the rear seat.

We would be flying CAP (combat air patrol) high over the Nevada desert, looking for bad guys. Our flight consisted of four F-15s, referred to as a 4-flight, that was divided into a lead aircraft with its wingman, and a second pair of aircraft that would follow in formation behind them. The Tub served as the wingman bringing up the rear of the flight. As occupant of the rear seat of the rear aircraft, I could observe them all.

The "rules of engagement" for this exercise included the requirement to maintain at least 200 feet between any two combatants, and that an aerial encounter with aircraft of the opposing force should include a maximum of four-on-four, or a total of no more than eight aircraft in a single "furball." The movie footage you see of WW1 aircraft swirling about one another in combat is a clear reminder that, back then, they were traveling at a snail's pace, compared to modern jet fighters. There was no radar. Every encounter was eyeballs and seat-of-the-pants flying.

At the Red Flag exercise, each aircraft sported its own powerful radar, capable of sighting moving objects many, many miles away— farther than human sight could discern. Each of them also broadcast an FOF (friend or foe) identifier. If the radar electronics did not detect a friendly FOF signal, then the cockpit display indicated its location as an unfriendly target.

We sighted an active furball of 4 friendlies and 4 unfriendlies. This was the previous mission that was scheduled to return to Nellis as we arrived. Rather than circle at a distance, waiting for them to return "home," we approached at combat air speed. This demonstrates the effect of a notion among fighter pilots, known as "the big sky" theory. There is so much sky out there, that the probability of a mid-air collision is small.

As we engaged the furball, converting it to eight-on-four. Every pilot eagerly sought the opportunity to rack up a "kill." It soon became obvious that our outnumbered opponents would be toast in no time.

Radars beeped and warned more urgently, competing with intermittent buzzing and beeping of potential stall warnings as well as over-G warnings. The new 4-flight of opponents had arrived on the scene.

The big sky was shrinking. There were good guys and bad guys in every direction, looping and rolling and pressing their aircraft to the limits. And they were close. At one point, an opposing aircraft was so close to my canopy that I could clearly see individual rivets on the underside of its wing, as it rolled and pulled out of our path.

I have no notion of how long our eight-on-eight furball lasted. My G-suit (a pressurized pair of pants that automatically responds to the G forces on the aircraft) had nearly crushed my femurs to powder. As a passive observer, it all occurred in an ever-surprising, slow motion. But then, abruptly, it was a four-on-four furball, with all participants dutifully observing the minimum safe distance.

19. North Rim Photo Op

1984

During the spring of 1984, my Squadron Commander asked me if I would be interested in attending the USAF Survival Training. I eagerly accepted. He arranged it for that summer. At the time, I did not understand why my mention of it to any of the squadron's fighter pilots elicited odd responses, like you might expect if you mention that your dog just died. Although I had attended a short survival training at Brooks AFB, during my aerospace medicine training, this was the real deal, at Fairchild AFB, outside of Spokane, Washington.

With some schedule juggling, I was able to drive my new Bronco II to Tucson, where my son, Micah—then 6 years old—was living with his mother and sister. I planned to drive with him to the Grand Canyon and back to Tucson, prior to boarding a flight to Spokane, to attend the survival training.

That training would begin with a delightful excursion into the Cascades, with detailed lectures on wilderness survival, as well as orienteering skills with map and compass. I've always enjoyed that sort of experience. What I had not expected, and what in retrospect was the source of the odd responses from members of my squadron, was that the second half of that lengthy training consisted of what was termed, "resistance training." This segment was taught by former POWs from the Viet Nam War. It was essentially training (by first-hand experience) for how to avoid captivity, or after capture, how to survive under extreme duress, while not revealing meaningful or valuable information.

The trainers were career goons and sadists. The content of the training is considered classified, but I can say clearly that there was no *physical* torture involved. It was one of the ugliest experiences of my entire life, though I did not come anywhere close to dying.

But...before going to that training, I picked up Micah in Tucson, and the two of us drove up for our first trip (of many) to the Grand Canyon. We began with a boat tour on Lake Powell, then drove down to the North Rim of the Grand Canyon.

For our entire trip, my Bronco II's cassette tape player was busy playing my tape collection of Jean Michel Jarre and Tangerine Dream. To this day both Micah and I still enjoy listening to their electronic music.

Entering the North Rim Lodge, I checked in at the reservations desk, while Micah wandered out to the south balcony. Neither of us had ever seen the Grand Canyon. When Micah returned, his jaw was spontaneously dropped—not as an intended affect. His eyes were wide. He had no words.

Then the two of us went on out to the rim itself, strolling along the trail at the top of the gorge. I carried my somewhat heavy, Minolta 35 mm camera. I set it to fully automatic focus and exposure, and showed him how to take a photo with it.

A ways out the trail, we came to a spot with a sculpted pedestal on the canyon side of the trail. I hopped over a 30" gap, onto the pedestal, leaned against its top stone, and suggested that Micah snap a photo of me.

It turned out to be a nicely framed photo of me, leaning on that stone pedestal, with a gorgeous view of that section of the Canyon in the background.

As I was about to hop back across that 30" gap, to where Micah waited with the camera, I gasped. Looking down it, I realized that a single misstep, and I would have fallen over 100 feet to the rocks below.

BRIGHT ANGEL
TRAIL

RIM TRAIL ➡

20. South Rim Nighttime Stroll

1984

Sometimes I am a slow learner. After a night in a log cabin on the North Rim, Micah and I spent a long day driving back eastward (more Jean Michel Jarre and Tangerine Dream), back across Navajo Bridge over the Colorado, then around to the South Rim of the Canyon. Driving between the Canyon's North Rim and South Rim is a lesson in the transition of ecology (the temperature, the plants and trees, the wildlife) that occurs from one elevation to another.

As I drove, I pondered something else that I had already decided, back at Eglin. Our fighter wing had a brand new flight surgeon—just joined the Air Force, and fresh out of his training in aerospace medicine. Somebody higher up had decided that a great introduction to Air Force life for a new physician would be a deployment to Saudi Arabia in December. The same place that left a sour taste in my mouth during my trip the previous year. As the wing's Senior Flight Surgeon, I decided that such a deployment would be the surest way for the Air Force to lose a promising physician, as soon as his first commitment ended. So I had suggested that I go then instead. My Wing Commander agreed.

So only a few months after this wonderful journey with Micah, I would watch the opening night of the 1984 movie, *Dune*, in Ft. Walton Beach, then fly the following morning to one of the bleakest parts of the world. The result of my second journey to Riyadh was that, upon my return, I was determined to leave the Air Force as soon as my commitment ended, which was June of 1985. I have regretted that decision ever since.

Although both rims look into the same canyon, the climate, scenery and even the aroma are completely different. In that one day, we drove from relatively cool, Aspen forests, abounding with greenery and occasional grassy meadows to the somewhat barren, desert plateau of the South Rim. We arrived at our lodging at sunset.

Once we were settled in, Micah and I strolled toward the center of the village along the rim road. Most Park Service functions were closed for the night. We passed the cemetery in which many the legendary pioneers of the Grand Canyon were buried. We had yet to look into the Canyon from the South Rim.

I saw a small sign to the South Rim Trail. As we strode down the asphalt path, looking for the South Rim Trail, we moved farther from the scantily lighted roadway, and into the near pitch black of the unlighted path. Micah began to cry.

I tried to encourage him. But Micah refused to go any farther in the darkness. A bit annoyed, I turned around, and we walked back to our lodging.

The following morning, we ate breakfast at one of the canteens, then headed back to walk that path to the South Rim Trail, first visiting the now-open Visitor Center, located just east of the cemetery. Then we located that same sign directing us to the South Rim Trail, now in bright daylight.

I recognized the point at which Micah had refused to continue the previous night. Twenty feet beyond where we had turned around in the darkness, the asphalt path intersected with the asphalt paved South Rim Trail. A few feet farther, without guard rail or fencing, the upper Kaibab cliff, which forms the rim, dropped hundreds of feet to the steep rocky slope of the Toroweap formation.

21. Copper Mountain White-out

1987

When I left active duty in the Air Force during the summer of 1985, I purchased a house on 10 acres of farmland southwest of Chicago, Illinois. I became a solo Pediatrician, in private practice. [That actually means that I started a small, for-profit business, expecting my young patients' families or their health insurance to provide my personal income, as well as cover all the substantial costs of operating that business. The parents themselves were often quite young, and uninsured.] I was appointed Chief of Pediatrics at our local hospital— an honor and responsibility that came with no additional income.

My son, Micah, then 7 years old, came to live with me. My sister, Lynn, also lived with us, and provided care for Micah when I was busy elsewhere. I planted a fruit orchard (35 trees), a grove of Carpathian walnuts (20 trees) and a grove of Chinese chestnuts (20 trees). I put in long rows of raspberries and Strawberry popcorn. We fished in our own pond, and grew vegetables. I planted varieties of blueberries and gooseberries.

Just to the west of my home, my neighbor continued to plant 40 acres of corn. To the east, a charming, wooded creek valley marked the property line. But just to the South, across the two-lane highway, sat the Country Club and its expansive golf course. I was ambiguously rural.

By the end of my first year of private practice, I had accumulated over $50,000 of receivables—billed services that had not been paid. My accountant and the administrators of the hospital urged me to submit those receivables to a collection agency. They suggested that I not accept any Medicaid patients. That's how it's done. I would not agree. My finances teetered. I could not (and subsequently never could) predicate my decisions to provide the best care I could to patients, solely based on their ability to come up with cash or its surrogate.

I was a dummy. I should have known in advance that plunging into America's long-entrenched, fee-for-service model of health care was not a way of life that I could accept. While I enjoy having money, I am a complete failure at billing for doing something that I love to do. I am a terrible businessman.

During the early spring of 1987—my second year of private practice, a married pair of physicians at our hospital staff, a pediatrician and an obstetrician (both natives of Poland), offered me the free use of a week of their spacious condominium time-share at the Copper Mountain Ski Resort in Colorado. I invited my brother, Richard, and his wife and daughter to join me. Then Micah—now 9— and I hopped into my Bronco II, and drove to Colorado.

One snowy morning, while Micah was in the hands of a kid's skiing class, I decided to ski down the mountain, from the highest lift. I was surprised that there was no line of skiers waiting to get on the lift. About half-way up, the buffeting winds whipped the fine, falling powder into a translucent whiteness. I could see each nearby lift tower that I passed, but nothing in front of me or below me. It was a white-out.

When I arrived at the top, the man-made structures were easy enough to make out, but I could not discern the surface of the snow on the ground from the falling snow that enveloped me. I knew, from the ski trail map, that somewhere off to my right, an easy, circuitous trail descended most of the mountain. If I skied beyond that trail head, there were hazardous trails and a descent into a bowl on the far side of the mountain.

I could see nothing. The deep powder hid my skis and boots half-way up to my knees. I crouched and snow-plowed as slowly as I could, allowing my tenuous feel of the slope angle, and gravity itself to guide me, as I crept downward, totally blind. After struggling for at least forty frightening minutes, I began to see trees again.

Over a dozen skiers died on Copper Mountain that year.

22. North Kaibab Trail Photo

1991

On my return trip from Copper Mountain in 1987, I decided to pause for several hours in Columbia, Missouri, to show Micah some of the wonderful places I used to enjoy there in the early 1970s. This turned out to be one of my life's great revelations.

The 100 acre farm north of town, belonging to a classmate, Lance, was now a subdivision. I drove south of town, to the farm where Rita and I had lived during my final 6 months in Columbia. The orchards, the pastures, the steep gravel driveway that crossed a creek: all of these were gone. More subdivision. When we are young, we seldom notice the slow but constant change that all places undergo. We perceive that people and animals and things change, and that places do not. But Siddhartha Gautama was correct. All things are impermanent, and sometimes startlingly so.

A decade later, Backpacker Magazine published an article about the surprising fact that within the entire continental United States, the greatest distance of any point on the map from the nearest road was 20 miles—and that was a rarity from a large, designated wilderness area. We always manage to alter the places we love.

In the summer of 1991, Micah's Boy Scout troop traveled to the Grand Canyon. They were divided into four groups, determined by skill level and physical capability. I hiked with Micah's group, which was hiking rim-to-rim-to-rim in 6 days. From the South Rim, we hiked down the South Kaibab Trail to the bottom in one day, then spent two days climbing the North Kaibab Trail to the higher, North Rim.

The heat was brutal, but we were well prepared. A foot off the ground above the red, Dox Formation, exposed near the bottom of the South Kaibab Trail, just before it plunges into the inner gorge, my little backpack thermometer registered 120°F (its maximum). That spot was where we regretted taking a 5 minute break from our descent. There is no shade at all, and the Canyon's Redwall cliff above, radiates like a toaster oven at mid-day.

Descending from the South Rim to the river in a single day, especially carrying a loaded backpack during the summer, sucks away every scrap of muscle energy. As hungry as we were after arriving at Bright Angel Campground, beside Phantom Ranch and the outlet of Phantom Creek, it felt like a major chore to pitch a tent, then light up a little camp stove for preparing dinner. Many of us chose to just sit in the middle of Phantom Creek, only afterwards discovering that tiny leeches had hitched onto our skin.

The lower portion of the North Kaibab Trail, our challenge for day two—to reach Cottonwood Campground, followed the creek valley, and was the gentlest slope that we ascended. It was too gentle. I recall our teen boys passing the early evening climbing high onto the steep, crumbly slopes to the west of the creek. They caused some minor rock slides, and a reprimand from the resident Park Ranger.

The great challenge for day three was ascending the Redwall, and then the more gradual slope up to the North Rim. At the very top of the Redwall, along the final hundred feet of trail prior to the wooded slopes below the Rim, we paused for a brief break.

Someone, I've forgotten who, wanted me to pose against a massive tree trunk, for a photo. That tree came up from somewhere below the level of the trail. I gave that little thought. With my heels at the edge of the Redwall cliff, I leaned back against the trunk. It's slow sway from my impact seemed odd to me. I smiled. The photo was taken, then I looked down.

My back was resting at about the halfway point of a 200 foot tall, Ponderosa pine trunk. There was nothing but a beckoning void to either side. The oscillating gap at my feet varied from about 2 inches to 8 inches.

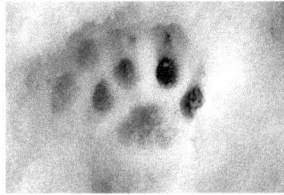

23. Dusk Visit to the Colorado Divide

1991

In October of 1991, I flew out to Aurora, Colorado, for a medical conference, paid for by my hospital's administration. The conference they chose was one aimed specifically at medical chairmen of hospital departments. That is not a subject that I personally would have chosen, but a free trip to Colorado is a free trip.

I rented a small, "compact" car from the airport in Denver, for my short excursions that surrounded the meeting sessions. I dutifully attended (and paid attention during) all the sessions of the modestly interesting presentations. Today, I have zero recollection of anything that was said or shown, during the low-light, slide-shows of graphs and charts and photos of smiling physicians in long white coats.

I rarely wore a white coat in my hospital. I steadfastly never wore a white coat within my office practice. One universal truth of pediatrics is that children, especially small children, are frightened by a white coat. A necktie was usually received as a neutral garment, whereas an open-collar, short-sleeve print shirt rated as friendly markings. When I did wear a necktie, I kept it tucked into my shirt, between the second and third buttons from the top. No sense wagging a filthy strip of unwashable cloth at every child.

My return flight from Denver was scheduled for a day after the conference ended. That was intentional on my part. I drove up to Boulder, to visit a few spots, then decided at mid-day, to drive west from Denver on the Interstate. Clearly marked on one of the many detailed maps I collect of every place that I visit or intend to visit, a road climbed up the western slope of the Front Range, and continued on down the eastern slope, crossing the Continental Divide along the way. What a great way to return to Denver for my flight home the following morning.

As this back road gradually traversed northward, it steadily climbed. The pavement ended. I stopped, and checked the map again. Yes. It subtly indicated that the road was no longer paved above a certain elevation. But it clearly showed the now unpaved road crossing the Divide, and descending toward Denver.

I eventually reached a mostly bald area at the top, including a rustic sign marking the Continental Divide. Yippie! The sun was still above the western horizon. But the road ahead—the road down the eastern slope, was deeply washed out. Only a high-clearance, four-wheel-drive vehicle would have a fighting chance of making it down. I would have to return along the same road I had just climbed.

I exited the little rental car, and walked about the Divide for a few minutes. Clouds swept in. It began to snow. As I pivoted to return to the car, I saw, in the fresh snow, the 5"-wide foot print of a feline. I spun around, but saw no mountain lion through the giant flakes falling heavily about me.

I quickly returned to the safety of my car, then began the much less secure process of descending an unpaved road that switchbacked down the western slope. The drive itself was low-speed, white-knuckle creeping, occasionally skidding in worrisome locations.

About half-way down, I reached the long stretch of straight traverse. I had to pee. I stopped, stepped out of the car, and peed into the now 6"-deep snow. Then I noticed, only a few feet from the car, another quite fresh, feline foot print.

Alarmed, I inspected the interior of the car, then hopped in, and slammed the door. Through the snow-tainted windows, I could see no mountain lion. Only then, did I consider the fact that no person on earth knew that I had driven up to the divide. Nobody would have noticed if I had failed to return. If I were injured, as opposed to killed and eaten, I simply would have been missing from Denver—for days.

24. Quiet Night alongside the Colorado River

1991

Backpacking successfully inside the Grand Canyon can become surprisingly addictive. As with any physical challenge undertaken in a rugged area or wilderness, advance knowledge and careful preparation minimize the probability of a poor outcome. With the rim-to-rim-to-rim hike during the summer of 1991 foremost in the minds of each of us who completed it, a more challenging Grand Canyon trek, this time during the much more comfortable weather of late December, was planned. I use the passive voice here, because I can no longer recall who initiated the idea. I do know that the backcountry permit request had to be submitted on the first day of September, prior to the planned hike. So after the Canyon trip in June, the permit request for yet another trek inside the Grand Canyon was submitted two months later.

This time, it would be limited to eight teenage boys and two adults. Also, the planned route would be along what the Park Service regards as an unimproved or wilderness trail, as opposed to the carefully maintained "tourist" trails—North and South Kaibab, and the Bright Angel Trail. We would be hiking the "Hermit Loop," which originates at the western extent of the Park's Rim Road, descends the Hermit Trail, then follows the Tonto Trail eastward to Indian Garden, which is half-way up the Bright Angel Trail from Phantom Ranch. It would be two days of driving each way, and five days of backpacking, scheduled within the Christmas break of 1991. We would be inside the Canyon on Christmas Day.

With ten of us traveling from Illinois, we rode in two vehicles. My new 1991 GMC Suburban towed a borrowed trailer, filled with gear.

We ultimately parked these in the parking lot at Hermits Rest. Since the Park Service limited "wilderness" campsites to a maximum of six people per night, I divided our group into two groups of five, and obtained permits for two relatively (in Grand Canyon terms) nearby campsites for each of the nights. For each side-canyon with somewhat easy access to the river (Hermit Creek, Monument Creek), one group would get to camp at the creek crossing on the Tonto Platform, while the other descended to the mouth of the creek at the Colorado River. Where that was not practical (Salt Creek, Horn Creek), one lucky group would get to hike on to the next stop, typically 4 trail miles farther.

When we first arrived at Hermit Creek, the group destined to stay there pitched its tents, while the others continued down to the river. Curiously, once the upper group had set up camp, they all decided to hike down to the river that evening anyway, and subsequently found themselves climbing back up the moderately difficult trail from the bottom of the inner gorge in total darkness, to get back to their tents. This bit of extra tribulation played a role in the events of the following day.

That second day was Christmas Eve. While Monument Canyon is just the "next side-canyon east" of Hermit, the hike itself follows the Tonto Trail, as it skirts along the edge of the high cliffs above the inner gorge. It is a strenuous walk, with full backpacks, no shade and a short, dead-of-winter day. Once the trail ascends the ridge separating the two side-canyons, it promptly descends to the upper creek bed of Monument Creek, where the Tonto Trail crosses it. The "upper" campsite is located there, beneath a convenient cliff overhang. The "stay at the upper campsite" group of the previous night would need to then descend another several miles down the generally friendly creek valley, to reach the lower campsite for the night, at Granite Rapids. There, I and they would pitch tents on the sandy beach alongside the Colorado.

My fellow adult, Tom, and I had planned a surprise Christmas Day celebration meal, but both of us were staggering under the weight of our overloaded backpacks. I was carrying a large can of candied yams, and several other heavy items for the Christmas menu. Tom's pack carried a 4-pound, canned ham, along with other heavy things. In a closed conference, we decided that Christmas Eve was the perfect time to eat our big Christmas dinner. Part of my burden was a string of Christmas lights, powered by two D-cell batteries. Unfortunately, nobody would be eating the batteries.

So the impromptu plan was to celebrate with the big meal at the upper campsite, then I would accompany the "lower campsite" group to the beach at the river. After a hasty, early breakfast by the river, we would climb back up, and rejoin the rest as they cleaned up after sleeping late, and enjoying their leisurely breakfast.

The Christmas Eve bash was a delight, complete with a decorated Christmas "tree", and the giving of small gifts. I think we might also have opened a bottle of sparkling cider. Then came the mutiny.

The first few days of every backpacking trip are always the most difficult. The group scheduled to now, after their Christmas Eve feast, hike several more miles, and set up camp by the light of their flashlights decided (it was a conspiracy!) to pitch their tents right there, at the upper campsite. I explained that it would violate our backcountry permits. They shrugged.

I informed them that I would certainly be heading down there, as soon as I got my backpack re-packed and strapped on. They shrugged.

Although 14 year old boys are not widely known for their tact, they at least waited until I had descended down the trail, and was out of sight, before setting up their tents. With my backpack noticeably lighter—some of its previous contents now residing in the bellies of the mutineers, I picked up my pace, and reached the Colorado River at dusk. The white noise of water sloshing continuously over Granite Rapids serenaded the pitching of my tent on the beach, among tamarisk and some tall grasses, within 10 feet of the water.

Back in 1991, whenever I was backpacking, I carried a folding, wind-up "travel alarm clock", mostly so that I could set its alarm, if I needed to awaken at a specific time. I had determined to awaken early enough to strike camp, and reach the upper campsite while all the mutineers were still sleeping.

As things turned out, I actually did not need that ¾-pound travel alarm. I awakened to pee during the early hours before dawn. I immediately sensed that the sound of Granite Rapids had changed. It was no longer a soothing melody, but a rather harsh, angry sounding rush. I slipped my feet into my boots, and unzipped the nylon door of my tan, Eureka Timberline-2, and saw sloshing water at the base of the tent. I grabbed a flashlight. There was water everywhere, except the back of the beach, slightly uphill from my tent. Worse, I could no longer see the trail along the beach, the one that had led from the mouth of Monument Creek to my campsite.

Without dressing, I pulled up the 8 tent pins, then, with my pack and sleeping bag and travel alarm clock still in the tent, I dragged the whole mess up the slight slope. I have never packed my backpack so carelessly, and with a soaking wet tent just bundled like rags, and lashed on. Then, still wearing just my Thermax long johns and my boots, I skirted the rushing, rising water, lugging my now even heavier backpack. I edged up the rocky slop as far as I could, rock-hopped onto some large boulders that were still above the water, and finally, with a solid rush of adrenaline, reached the still quiet mouth of Monument Creek. I climbed up the trail a short distance, then stopped. I dumped out my soaking backpack, and dressed in my now damp clothing, though I retrieved dry underpants and socks from their Ziploc bags. I shook off as much water from the tent as I could, then repacked everything in its habitual, tidy arrangement.

After climbing partway by flashlight, then the remainder by the predawn light, I arrived at the upper campsite just as the mutineers were beginning to stir. I had decided to act as if nothing exceptional had occurred. But when Tom asked me how it was down there, I spilled the beans.

Periodically, the operators of Glen Canyon Dam, upstream from the Colorado within the Grand Canyon, would issue a notice that they would be "flushing" the river. Like flushing a giant commode, they open the gates of the dam, and allow the torrent to "scrub the beaches, and renew the historic ecology of the river. They nearly scrubbed me from the beach.

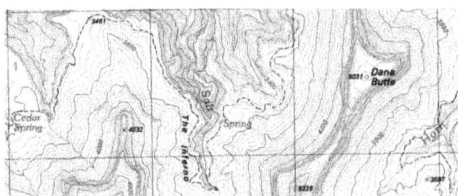

25. Salt Creek Pour-off

1991

Reading a topographic map is a relatively straightforward task for most areas of the country. Each meandering, brown line indicates a constant elevation. Darker brown lines also display that elevation (in feet or meters above sea level). So a knoll appears as a target shape of wiggly rings, each higher elevation "ring" smaller than the one below it. Topographic maps that indicate a cliff may show several distinct rings that converge at the steepest portion of the cliff.

But the Grand Canyon is a warren of cliffs like few other places on earth. Some of them may drop nearly straight down thousands of feet. So in those cliff areas, one can count up the number of converging lines, to get an estimate of just how high (or how far a drop) one might encounter at that cliff.

The Tonto Platform, which appears from the South Rim to be the bottom of the Canyon, but with a vicious, dendritic crack across the length of it, is an undulating slope of limestone and shale layers, all resting on the pie-crust-like sandstone of the Tapeats. It is the Tapeats that rims the upper edge of the 900 foot drop into the granite of the Inner Gorge—the near vertical walls of the Colorado River through much of its course within the Canyon.

I'll admit that the topographic map of the Grand Canyon is, for me, a mess to read adequately. I'm pretty good at identifying the hallmarks of "cliff," "big cliff," "really big cliff," and "holy crap, that's a big cliff." For Salt Creek, I could see a "big cliff" partway down the bed of the creek. If a lot of water were flowing down such a creek, the big cliff in the bed would be a spectacular waterfall. Given the usually scant flow of Salt Creek (It's canyon is nicknamed, "The Inferno"), that same cliff is referred to as a "pour-off."

The Tonto Trail segment between Monument Creek and Salt Creek skirts the edge of the Tapeats cliff, with beautiful (i.e. terrifying) views into the Inner Gorge along much of its length. Then, as with the Tonto Trail in most of the side-canyons, it wends its way toward the head, as it drops down to the creek valley itself.

It was Christmas Day. Our "two" groups were now hiking as a single entourage, with the assumption that we would also camp together each night for the remainder of the hike through Indian Garden and the climb back to the South Rim. My plan to observe the backcountry permit rules had clearly failed.

The views from the creek crossing campsite in Salt Creek are stunning. To the South, a cup of staggering, seemingly vertical cliffs separated us from the rest of the world—the South Rim. Looking northward, I was presented with a winding, narrow gouge through the sandstone layers of the pie-crust Tapeats. Its bed curved out of sight about 100 yards from the trail crossing. The seep of water within Salt Creek came to the surface in the form of shallow pools, just before the drop-off. That would be our source of water for the next 24 hours. To pass the pools required the centrifugal force of sprinting along the curved walls above them.

Micah and five other boys wandered down with their water bottles. I followed with my own. The stretch of creek that directly led to the pour-off lay within a steep groove of oddly out of place, pure granite, scattered here and there with an isolated cactus—barrel cactus, prickly pear—struggling from cracks in the stone. The granite slopes to either side rose about 40 feet above the bed.

The boys approached the pour-off with enthusiasm, scrambling the western slope of granite, to get a better view into the Inner Gorge. This was accompanied by some swearing, and backing away. It seemed that while the pour-off was clean and abrupt, the granite slopes to either side sloped downward toward the precipitous drop. Micah lay on his belly, and scooted to the edge, to launch a wad of spit. He began to slip forward on the smooth surface, and shouted for someone to grab him. I was within about 15 feet of him, and lurched forward, grabbing his lower shin. I hauled him back from the edge.

Every year, people die at the Grand Canyon. A small percentage of them were hiking within the Canyon with inadequate preparation or knowledge of the risks presented—carrying inadequate water, carrying too much weight, heart attacks from inadequate physical preparation. But the preponderance of deaths comes from casual tourists doing foolish things at the Rim.

Most of the well-visited views along the South Rim are now provided with simple guard rails, yet tourists sometimes decide that a better selfie photo can be snapped by dipping under the rail, and moving just a little bit closer to the brink of the mile-deep, ten-mile-wide chasm. Some of those who die doing this fall from the cliff by dutifully following the instructions of a companion or family member holding a camera, who advises that they "back-up" just a bit more for a better photo.

More often, the fatal plunge is the result of the victim not recognizing that their secure footing rests upon loose scree or smooth stone that gently slopes toward the cliff drop. Once you begin to slide, there is nothing to grab, no anchor to save you from a careless death. Others will have to retrieve your mangled body.

Our group of boys and adults was experienced in hiking within the Canyon, though most of that experience had been on the wide, well groomed "tourist" trails that crossed the Canyon between the Grand Canyon Village, on the South Rim, and the North Rim Lodge and campgrounds. Only our two previous days of backpacking had been over "unmaintained" trails.

A curious phenomenon is how the brain, in only a few days, becomes accustomed to regarding the sometimes scarcely discernible trace of a crumbled scree path through the cacti and blackbrush as a meaningful trail. This mental adjustment is startlingly apparent the moment one steps from days on the Tonto Trail onto what seems like a four-lane highway of the Bright Angel Trail—the juncture at Indian Garden.

So after only those three days of hiking primitive trails (originally engineered by feral donkeys that once roamed the Canyon during the early 20th century), our brains had come to regard the profoundly hazardous slopes near the Salt Creek pour-off as ordinary.

My response to the teenagers' backing away from the brink was one of mild amusement at their timidity. I should have recognized that this group of backpack-hardened hikers had recognized a genuine danger. My son had tempted fate, as teenagers too often do.

I surveyed the area of the drop-off. The eastern granite slope had been too steep to ascend, whereas the western slope had seemed more approachable. After my unexpected effort to grab Micah's leg, I found myself in an equally precarious situation.

What I failed to perceive were the deceptive, complex slopes of this *saddle point*, and the utter lack of traction of my boots on the sloped granite. As I cautiously backed away down the left slope, the point where I felt safe (on one curve of the geometry—the 'U' shape of the creek bed) was actually beyond the safe point (on the other curve of the geometry—the bed's drop into the Inner Gorge). My slight sideways slippage on the granite, toward the creek bed increasingly sloped into the pour-off. I braced my foot on a small barrel cactus, which momentarily halted my slide. This allowed me to scoot backwards just enough so that, when the barrel cactus lost its purchase in the crack a moment later, and tumbled over the precipice, I did not follow it into oblivion.

Proof of our survival is my laughter-filled phone call with Micah 31 years later, to clarify the details of this episode. He rated it as the scariest moment of his life. He never did get to see that wad of spit vanish into the Inner Gorge.

Topographical maps, even the very best, fail to present slopes the way that the soles of my boots encounter them, one step at a time.

26. Big Sky Double Diamond Run

1992

In early spring of 1992, I drove my GMC Suburban from Illinois to a conference of the Wilderness Medical Society—of which I was a member, at the Big Sky Ski Resort in southwestern Montana, visiting Mount Rushmore along the outbound trip. The drive one way is a two day drive (12 hours each day) mostly along poker-straight, Interstate Highways all the way to Bozeman. The weather was lovely for the entire drive, other than a bit of light snow at Mount Rushmore. I listened to a little bit of radio as I drove, but mostly Tangerine Dream and Jean Michel Jarre tapes.

The conference itself resembled no other medical conference I had attended over the previous two decades. We were presented with grizzly bear attacks, and even a video of a grizzly being clocked at over 30 mph while chasing down an antelope. There were parasites and pathogens, injuries and hazards. Emphasis was on impromptu bandages and splints and stretchers, as well as preparations and precautions. (One speaker, a physician veteran of an Everest expedition, still had varicose veins on his eyelids.) The conference sessions filled each morning—all counting toward our mandated, continuing medical education hours, but leaving the afternoons and evenings free for skiing and excursions.

During one session, we all took a ski lift up the mountain to attend a class on snow avalanche risk assessment, the building of emergency snow shelters and igloos, and ski area emergency rescue. Wonderful stuff. The follow-on, indoor session discussed avalanche risk in detail, and even displayed photo slides of a particularly avalanche prone ski run at Big Sky, that would aim its snow tsunami directly at one particular cluster of condos built at its bottom end.

All of these hypothetical scenarios and possible remedies, while fascinating to contemplate, were just registering in my brain as academic content, albeit interesting academic content. Maybe some distant day in the future, some pearl of wisdom might turn out to be useful to me during a yet to imagine set of circumstances.

Avalanches are sneaky things. While an avalanche requires accumulated snow, several other key factors must come together in the right timing to cause that accumulated snow to suddenly break free as a layer, and slide down the slope, endangering people and property. It is temperature swings between separate snowfall events that create those identifiable layers, together with the overlying weight of one layer upon the next. And radiant warmth from the underlying rock or soil. Strange but predictable phase changes (to the snow / ice / water / water vapor) come about within each static layer of snow. If one surface of a snow layer, say the lower surface, is slightly warmer than the opposite surface—the upper surface—of the layer, perhaps due to radiant heat from the underlying rock, then the scant water vapor that escapes from the warmer surface, migrates to the cooler surface, and condenses there as either liquid water or as ice. The various physical phases of water play musical chairs.

From what I understood during the session on avalanches, the highest risk times were following multiple, heavy snowfalls during the springtime in the mid-afternoon. The conference was in the springtime, after multiple, heavy snowfalls. I was free to ski during the afternoons.

I was also free to do other things. One afternoon, I drove north to a Nordic skiing location, carrying my own cross-country boots, skis and wax. I actually enjoy the relative isolation and contemplative pace of Nordic skiing to the always overcrowded, theme park like lines and rides that are intrinsic to Alpine skiing. Nordic skiing is more strenuous, more personal, more satisfying.

I had first learned to Alpine ski while stationed in Germany, on a trip to Berchtesgaden. Nearly a decade later, sitting in my living room in Illinois, I had watched a VCR tape of how to Nordic ski. I think I watched that tape from end to end a dozen times. I read books about it. Then I purchased a pair of cross-country skis and boots, and learned to Nordic ski on winter hiking trails at state parks in northern Illinois. So I was essentially a self-taught skier in both forms. Lots of magazine articles, lots of books, and lots of self-confidence.

Two evenings during my stay at Big Sky, I drove down to a restaurant that specialized in bison meat. The burger on the first visit was wonderful. The ribeye on the second visit was one of the toughest steaks I have ever eaten.

On the afternoon following all the wilderness medicine discussions of avalanches, I rode the lifts up the mountain, and skied down mostly intermediate slopes, and occasionally the more difficult, black diamond slopes. It was fun, though I always find myself resenting the fact that Alpine ski boots and their bindings will not permit me to lift my heel. That arrangement is fine for going downhill, but a severe handicap when attempting to move under my own power over level snow. And it makes it nearly impossible to go uphill using my muscles.

On my second or third lift trip up the mountain that afternoon, I decided to follow markers to a different cluster of groomed slopes than the ones I had been skiing. If I approached a sign pointing to a particular slope, but it looked way too steep for me, I would glide on past, and check the head of the next marked slope. I eventually found one that seemed to be not as scary as the others, and started down that ski "trail". Somehow, my mind today refuses to remember the name of that otherwise indelible descent. I do recall that only later that day did I realize it was designated as a "double-diamond" slope.

As I glided happily past the point of no return, the slope became progressively steeper—too steep for my skiing skills. I began to zig-zag traverse at as shallow a descent angle as I could manage. The slope, impossibly, became even steeper. At that point, in order to traverse, my downhill leg was fully extended, while the knee of my uphill leg was nearly touching my chin. I was terrified.

Then, whoosh! A skier from higher on the slope sailed over my head. I managed to come to a full stop, and leaned my shoulder against the slope to rest. Whoosh! Whoosh! One after another, more skiers flew over me, vanishing below. I decided to remove my skis, and side-step my way (in my rigid boots) over to the side of the slope, and down.

It took me about 20 minutes to descend far enough to permit a view of the remainder of that ski run. I was dumbfounded. Not only did the slope's elevation drop many, many hundreds of feet to its end, the slope below was crisscrossed by bright orange snow fencing, with the presumption that skiers would jump the fences at high speed. And that they did. It was a multi-obstacle jumping run.

After I tore my eyes from the spectacle of skiers soaring through the air, landing between snow fences at high speed, then launching again over the next obstacle, I turned my gaze at what lay just beyond the very bottom of the ski run. It was the exact camera angle of the color slide from the avalanche session—"a particularly avalanche prone ski run at Big Sky, that would aim its snow tsunami directly at one particular cluster of condos built at its bottom end."

I was sweating from exertion. The afternoon had warmed. Conditions were perfect for an avalanche. My heart pounded.

Sideways step by awkward sideways step, I descended the brutal slope. At each of the snow fences, I would hug the downhill side of the bright plastic, my head ducked, and traverse far enough to go around the end of the snow fence below it. All the while, I was also lugging my skis in my hands, sometimes dragging them, sometimes using them as supports. My two ski poles dangled free at my wrists by their wrist straps.

About 2/3 of the way to the bottom, I noticed an occasional high-speed skier below me suddenly traverse off to my left, and vanish into the towering trees. As I neared that curious point in the slope, I saw that there was a connecting trail—a gently descending one—that wended its way to somewhere else. When I reached it, I stepped into my ski bindings and skied away to somewhere that was not threatening. I can no longer remember its end point. But it was close to the conference center.

That whole ordeal, with threats of decapitation by ski, broken bones and avalanche were all the result of my poor choice of a ski trail suitable for my skill at skiing.

27. Outrunning the Blizzard at 80 mph

1992

By the end of the Wilderness Medical Society conference in Big Sky, Montana, I had become aware of the forecast for a snow storm that would slowly sweep across the upper mid-west. It would start near the western slope of the Rockies, and move eastward over the following two days. I set out in the morning, on dry roads, for my two day drive back to Illinois.

For this trip, I was driving my 1991 GMC Suburban, with a 350 cubic-inch V-8 engine and 4-wheel drive. On the highway, I usually kept it in two-wheel drive, with the front hubs unlocked—for the best gas mileage. On this run, knowing a snow storm would soon be on my heels, I locked the front hubs, just in case I might need the 4-wheel drive with little notice.

My Suburban was a beast in snow. Nothing had ever been too deep or too slippery for it to handle, even in the "Chicago" winter. There had been occasions when I would stop by the roadside, bring out my towing cable, and tow a stranded motorist's Jeep out of a snow-filled road shoulder ditch. I seldom gave its performance a second thought. It was a capable vehicle.

The return drive through Montana was under crisp, blue skies, though the temperature hovered in the 20s. I tended to drive on Interstate highways in those days at about 5 mph above the posted speed limit. And the posted limit in that part of the country, with its flat, relatively straight Interstates was already higher than in most of the rest of the country. State Troopers in every state that I knew of would not blink an eye, unless a motorist exceeded the posted speed limit by at least 10 mph. Over a span of 10 hours of driving, that extra 5 mph would shorten the drive time by about an hour. That's meaningful, so long as it's safe.

A study of drivers in 2022 (30 years after this event) found that in conditions of heavy rain or snow, most drivers drove more carefully, and at a speed slower than they would ordinarily drive if the road conditions were dry. There was an exception to that tendency, they noted. It seems that middle-aged males tended to not reduce their speed for heavy rain or snow, but just cruised at their usual, clear weather speed. This was in contrast to the behavior of younger male drivers as well as more elderly male drivers, who were more inclined to exercise greater caution when driving in challenging conditions.

I was 42, nearly 43 years old when I was returning from Montana. I was driving my reliable beast. As I crossed the north-east corner of Wyoming, the snow storm began to overtake me. Ha! My front hubs were already locked. Without even slowing down, I shifted into 4-wheel drive, and continued on.

The snow accumulated. I found that at times, I would briefly feel a decrease in traction. To remedy that, I would shift back into two-wheel drive, so that the deceleration traction would instantly straighten out my path. I would soon return the gearbox to 4-wheel drive. I sailed along.

Shortly after crossing the state boundary into South Dakota, I realized that a State Trooper was following me at a distance, with all of his lights flashing. I shifted back into two-wheel drive, and gradually slowed to a speed that allowed me to safely pull onto the shoulder, and stop.

The Trooper got out, and stomped up to my lowered window. He was white as a ghost, and furious. He wore Wyoming insignia. He immediately shouted to me that he was scared to death trying to get me to stop, and that he nearly spun-out twice.

"You're driving through this snow like a crazy man!"

I explained that I was trying to out-run the storm. He was not impressed. He also could not issue me a ticket in South Dakota.

I drove, slowly, to the next exit, and spent the night at a motel. The next morning I drove cautiously in the now much deeper snow.

28. Freight Train vs. Rental Truck with Car Trailer

1993

During the middle of the 19th century, some towns and many counties across America began to establish local poor farms. These provided simple housing and food for those in the community deemed indigent or enfeebled, or simply too old to still provide for their own needs. It was the 1800s idea of social security. Most of the county-run (and funded) poor farms were located well beyond the bounds of a town, and consisted of a rather nice house for the director, a still reasonably comfortable, nearby house for the superintendent or manager, and a collection of typically single-room houses (or as two-room duplexes) for each of the residents. A tiny house.

The poor farm might or might not engage in some form of agriculture or animal husbandry, to offset costs. Regardless, the residents paid nothing for their room and board.

Poor farms began to fade away once the nation's Social Security act was signed in the 1930s, with the last disappearing in the early 1950s. They are now either "historic" sites or just common farmland.

In the summer of 1993, I closed my practice, and planned move to southwest Virginia, to join my eldest brother, Richard, in his growing computer business. I sold my GMC Suburban, keeping my 1984 Bronco II. I sold my house. Micah and I packed up everything into a giant rental truck (a moving van). My intention was to rent a house.

In Virginia, Richard had located a lovely, two bedroom home for me in a secluded nook in a rural county north of Blacksburg. It had once been the superintendent's house of the county's long forgotten poor farm.   Adjacent was the former Director's larger house, now inhabited by a high school teacher and her son. Curiously, at the back of "my" fenced-in yard stood the only remaining building for poor farm residents, a twenty foot long storage shed, that had two doors, each opening into a single room.

To get my Bronco II to come east with me, I rented a car trailer that would carry the Bronco II behind the huge rental truck. We departed early in the morning, for the 10+ hour drive. We visited briefly with my younger brother, Jon, and his family, then living in Ohio, and continued on to Virginia.

My list of specific directions to the poor farm concluded with, "Take the last road to the left, before you reach the river." On that penultimate road, a paved one, I missed the turn onto a poorly marked, gravel road, and continued down a curving descent. As I crossed a set of railroad tracks with the giant rental truck, car trailer in tow, I saw the New River in front of me. The pavement ended after the tracks, and continued as a dirt, river road, ten feet from the edge of the water.

I stopped the truck, which was half-way across the tracks, and began to back up—with the body of the truck obscuring my view of the car transport trailer. On my third or fourth attempt to align the trailer with the paved road behind me, I spotted a bright light in the distance, centered above the tracks. There were no crossing lights or gates there. Just tracks. A gazillion-car coal train was zooming toward me. It blew its air horns, without slowing.

In a desperate act of faith in the power of the rental truck's engine, I placed the gears in reverse, then stomped the accelerator to the floor. I could see that the car trailer had fully rotated to my left, and could hear its metal hitch groaning against the rear of the truck. But the front end of the rental truck was nonetheless backing off the tracks.

At the moment when the diesel locomotive whizzed past, there was only about a foot of clearance between the nearest corner of the truck and the seemingly endless procession of freight cars.

29. Just a Quick 4-Mile Run at age 48

1996

Our house on the poor farm was a cozy, comfortable home: two bedrooms, a kitchen, living room, bath, enclosed back porch, and a breezy, open front porch that looked out to a gentle valley of a five acre pasture, grazed by cattle and miniature horses. A massive, silver maple tree shaded the front yard. The well fenced yard was entered by a swinging, livestock gate. The half-acre yard included two bearing fruit trees, and my vegetable garden in the back corner, alongside the remnant, duplex shed that had once served as a residence for two indigent people.

While wandering the borders of the pasture, I located evidence of several, slightly sunken, unmarked grave sites. The poor farm would bury its dead at county expense, which did not include a stone marker. I suspect that no records still exist of how many poor farm residents were buried out there.

Having grazing cattle and miniature horses as an immediate neighbor offers a few drawbacks, but many wonderful hours of observation and interaction. On the drawback side of things, the horses had somehow acquired the habit of scraping a bit of paint off any car parked outside the gate to my yard. It seems they liked the taste of it. And since my mailbox was about 50 yards beyond my yard gate, on a dirt drive across the corner of the pasture, there was always the need to watch my step, to avoid cow pies.

At times, when I would approach the fence that separated me from the pasture, one specific, young heifer—mostly cream-colored, with a scattering of light brown—would directly approach me. She brought along an entourage of flies that would circle about her head and her butt. It seems she was accustomed to a human scratching her chin and her face, and went out of her way to solicit that attention. I found it a bittersweet sort of bonding, knowing that her charming, pastoral life, and eager human interaction, was destined to end at a slaughterhouse.

In the spring of 1996, Micah was on the verge of graduating from high school, and deciding on what to do next. With several abrupt changes of heart, he seemed to have settled on entering the US Navy, hoping to pass the test for training as a Navy Seal. No doubt, Richard Marcinko's book, *Rogue Warrior*, play a decisive role in that decision. What teenager wouldn't want to defiantly crawl in the mud, freeze in the surf, and drink cobra venom?

So we canceled his plan to attend a diesel and automotive training program in northern Ohio, and focused on the goal of Navy Seal. First on the preparation agenda was the published physical standards required for the training. It is a daunting list of physical abilities and their minimum performance to qualify. Micah began to work out more strenuously. It was April.

In order to encourage him, I immediately quit smoking cigarettes, a habit that I had acquired, of all places, in medical school. I quit cold-turkey. Back in my early twenties, I discovered premium cigars and English-style pipe tobaccos. But during my year of cross-country motorcycle journeys on my Honda-450 Scrambler, which possessed only a 1-hour gas tank, I began smoking a cigarette at each stop.

The smoke from cigars and pipe tobacco is more alkaline (a higher pH) than that of cigarettes. This enables the nicotine to be absorbed through membranes of the mouth and nasopharynx. And their strength discourages inhaling the smoke into one's lungs. By contrast, the smoke of cigarettes is (almost by design) more acidic, and its nicotine is not absorbed in any appreciable amount, unless the smoke is drawn into the lungs. This renders cigarettes not only far more addictive than cigars and pipe tobacco, but directly damages the delicate alveoli of the lungs. But cigarettes were inexpensive (23 cents a pack) and convenient for a short break. And they required no paraphernalia, such as a cigar cutter or a pipe tamper and pouch, etc.

When I halted my cigarette smoking, I spent several weeks coughing up all the accumulated crud from my lungs, previously trapped there by the paralysis of airway cilia (the tiny "hairs" that propel foreign particles up and out of the airways) caused by cigarette smoking. Once that was generally cleared out, the cough vanished.

I also began to work out, and once again jog regularly. One hundred sit-ups, one hundred push-ups, fifty knee-bends and twenty chin-ups on a bar—every day. I had no personal aspiration to become a Navy Seal, but as an increasingly soft, middle-age man, I felt truly wonderful about restoring my physical fitness.

Three days a week, I would jog out the dirt driveway, dodging cow pies, and then turn down the gravel road, continuing until I reached the paved road that led down to the river (or uphill, into town).

I cannot recall that Micah ever joined me in my exercises or my jogging. I do remember his general absence from the house during his free time from school. Whether seeing his old man pretending to be a young man engendered any motivation or just amusement is hard to answer now, decades later. Both my memories and his have now been swayed by subsequent events and retrospection.

History is like that. We recall what was meaningful, rather than exact details. We carry away lessons, instead of facts. In the absence of a daily, detailed journal, impressions are all we are left with.

As the spring weather improved, I found myself running longer distances on each of my runs—still three days each week. At first, I would turn onto the paved road, and run uphill as far as our tiny post office, then turn around and run back home. One day, I used my car's trip odometer to measure half-mile intervals from my front yard, noting the structures or road signs at each of those points, up to two miles from home.

A few times I jogged much farther. And, of course, the total distance, round-trip, was double the marked distance. So I likely did a few runs of five or six miles on some of my jogging days. And I gradually increased my pace on each run. Over a span of a month of jogging, I began to feel as capable and as fit as I did when I used to regularly jog around Okaloosa Bay and Fort Walton Beach, during my Air Force days at Eglin.

Now 48, I felt as physically conditioned as I had felt in my mid-thirties. Micah, on the other hand, had discovered that he had red-green color "blindness", which disqualified him from becoming a Navy Seal. His enthusiasm for the Navy waned, though he did enlist after graduation.

But his initial desire to improve his fitness had transformed me. I was unstoppable.

On one of my jogging days, three weeks before Micah's scheduled graduation from high school, the temperature reached into the high 90s, with very high humidity. I didn't give that a second thought. I was up to the challenge. I had planned to run in mid afternoon to the two mile marker (nearly all uphill), then return (nearly all downhill). I ran in jogging shorts and a sleeveless t-shirt.

The heat was brutal all the way to the two mile marker. I turned around, and began the downhill return to our house. About half-way there, I experienced the odd sensation of suddenly having expended all my energy. It was as though the power line had been cut. My gait became shorter, as I plodded back home.

Once I passed through the fence gate, and into my front yard, all I could manage to do was to spread myself out on the cool grass in the shadow of the massive silver maple. I could hardly sit up. So I just lay there. I vaguely recall Micah and one of his friends passing me as they left the house, and commenting on how exhausted I appeared.

I experienced no chest pain. But as I cooled in the shade, my shortness of breath persisted. I eventually stumbled into the house, and pulled out my blood pressure cuff and stethoscope. Super-high blood pressure, double my normal, resting heart rate, and increasing, crackly rales in both my lungs. I was in heart failure.

I had experienced a painless heart attack. I rummaged through my trove of medications, took some Lasix, and located a large bottle of Diamox capsules (that I had purchased to minimize the hypoxia I experienced on high mountain peaks). That was my "therapy". I determined to treat my own heart attack. Somehow, I survived.

30. Night-Hike to Warspur in a Blizzard

1997

As I write this in 2022, I can say definitively that my heart has been incapable of beating any faster than 120 beats per minute, ever since that heart attack in 1996. That is my exercise limit. If it requires higher octane, I can't do it.

In the days after the heart attack, I found it physically challenging to walk as far as my mailbox. At work, a long stairway separated the parking lot from the front door. Descending it in the morning was easy, but climbing back up to the parking lot required my pausing every few steps.

A mere three weeks after my foolishly self-inflicted heart attack, Micah graduated from high school. Family members from around the country came for the occasion. When I look at the photos of that celebration today, I see myself as a well-dressed ghost, white as a sheet, prancing around in a three-piece suit. Off Micah went, to the Navy.

Two weeks later, I moved to a different house, which would have been impossible without the generous assistance of many friends and family. That is, they did all the work. I was incapable of carrying more than a few pounds at a time, and my living room bookcases shelved hundreds of books. The attic held probably another thousand books, all in large boxes.

I set about my own cardiac rehab program. Three mornings each week, before work, I would go to Blacksburg's indoor swimming pool, to swim laps. Since the water cooled my body during the exertion, it save my heart the added chore of pumping more blood into my skin to cool me. At first, I could comfortably swim only a single lap.

After three months, I could do thirty, quitting only because of a lack of time.

I walked. I took gradually lengthening strolls each evening in my new, rural neighborhood. Each Sunday morning, I would drive up to Mountain Lake, park the car, and hike along the dirt road, graduating to the hiking trails, including segments of the Appalachian Trail that passed through there. Sometimes I would walk into the nearby town and back.

By the early winter of 1997, I was departing from work each Friday evening, driving to some remote spot with my backpacking gear, and not returning to civilization until mid-day on Sunday. I had reached a point of endurance that enabled me to backpack with 40 pounds on my back. The limitation was strenuous, uphill climbs. My rehabilitated heart was still unable to exceed 120 beats per minute. So for those inevitable uphills, representing 50% of all hiking, I slowed my pace, and rested whenever I needed to.

My relationship with the weather when I backpacked would never entail a question of whether or not I should hike, but dictated what clothing I wore and carried. Rain or shine, fair or stormy, I always hiked as planned.

I suppose that the same attitude is what got me into trouble on that 4-mile run. But with backpacking in the nearby forests (much of it in the Washington and Jefferson National Forests in southwest Virginia), I always had the options of pitching my tent almost anywhere along my planned path, or even just turning around, and going back to my car. I never did either of those.

One advantage of planning a short backpacking trip in Virginia is that about a quarter of the entire length of the Appalachian Trail is located within the state. And in the tapered, southwestern portion of Virginia, where I was living, the hundreds of miles of the AT were only a relatively short drive from home. (The greatest risk was having to leave my parked car in very remote areas of very rural counties. Another risk was locking my car keys in the car in such a location—something that I perhaps did on one occasion—just one.)

An activity that I had enjoyed for years was to walk along a wooded trail at night, without the light of a flashlight. I would listen to the undisturbed sounds of wildlife, and find my way by the crunch of the footpath, its slope, and the change of texture when stepping into the surrounding duff. It takes only about 20 minutes of near-total darkness for the parts of the human retina that detect can only black and white—no color—to begin to function well, following exposure to typical human lighting environments. Then an unlit nighttime becomes a twilight of shadows and silhouettes. The stars sparkle. Walking a trail in darkness requires setting aside fears of unexpected (usually quite improbable) dangers. The ears become more important than the eyes.

Deer can be identified by the sounds of their hoofs on the duff, and an occasional snort. Raccoons will noisily climb the nearest tree, and growl from above. There are dangerous things out there, such as a surprised black bear, or an even more unlikely mountain lion. But my encounters with bears have been limited to identifying their feces, and then making an effort to be noisier (sometimes singing) as I continued along.

One Friday, my plan was to drive to a spot where an unpaved, country road crossed the AT. I would park there, then backpack entirely downhill, to spend the night at the Warspur shelter, situated at the far side of a broad valley of creeks and rhododendrons, in one of southwest Virginia's most rural of counties.

The weather forecast was for an inch of snow overnight. I dressed accordingly. I brought along a pair of very basic, short, instep crampons that would attach to my boots with two hefty rubber bands. By the time I had driven up to the spot where I had planned to park, a light snowfall had already begun.

I parked, strapped on my backpack and the crampons, and started down the AT (nominally south). Once my eyes had adjusted to the darkness, the white paint blazes marking the route of the AT sparkled brightly against the dark conifer trunks.

The snowfall became a heavy snow shower, accumulating rapidly. I continued in darkness, determined to not bring out my flashlight.

Even in the darkness and the falling snow, I could plainly see that a massive oak tree had recently blown down, completely blocking the trail. Passing below its sizable root ball would send me down a steep side slope. I chose to go upslope, and around the tree trunk and branches. This one unexpected detour consumed perhaps thirty minutes, as the snow accumulation continued.

The wind picked up, whipping through the tall conifers and the leafless hardwood trees. Snow began to adhere to the trunks of the trees. Before long, the painted, white blazes marking the trail were no longer identifiable amid the snow-caked trunks. I continued by the feel of the now snow-covered trail, hampered by the awkward hump of the instep crampons. Being able to remain upright was the singular blessing of my twin, Leki trekking poles.

I continued to descend. I had hiked this same route in the past, and knew from experience, as well as from the trail map, that it was a relatively short distance to the Warspur shelter. But after two hours of slogging through the deepening snow in the darkness, finding my way by the handicapped soles of my boots, I had still not reached the bottom of the slope. [As usual, nobody knew where I would be hiking.]

When I did reach the first creek crossing, I was impressed by how truly difficult it was to ascend two wooden steps up to the wooden trail bridge, especially wearing those wobbly, always slipping sideways rubber band crampons. Then three steps to descend at the other end. All in near total darkness. Way darker than a typical night hike.

I crossed the valley, and entered the forest at the far side, often having to backtrack to regain the lost trail. Then I came to the second creek crossing. The rock-strewn creek roared beneath the trail bridge, which consisted of three round, snow-covered logs, as its treadway. I could only feel the snow there in the blackness.

I unfastened my backpack's hip belt, and unhooked the chest strap that tethered to two pack straps together. If I fell into the creek, I wanted to not be attached to my pack. The logs were too high above the water for my trekking poles to reach a purchase on the rocks in the creek. Still in blacker than black darkness, I stepped sideways onto the center log, then inched my way across, stabilized only by a trekking pole to either side. My crampon points dug into the wood.

When I finally reached the Warspur shelter at about 2 am, it was deserted by humans, but hosted a jubilant party of hungry rats.

31. Escalante Route—a Tiny Ice Patch

1998

In the spring of 1997, I decided to complete a 5-day backpacking trek from the ridge south of Burkes Garden, Virginia, following the AT all the way to Pearisburg, Virginia. It would be my longest hike since my heart attack in May of 1996. My eldest brother, Richard would join me.

I had two custom ball caps embroidered, with letters on the front saying "Just Walkin' Home". As things turned out, Richard became ill just prior to the hike, so his wife, Diane, drove me to my starting point, and I set out alone. Along the way, many through-hikers sailed past me. I moved at my own pace, reaching the campsite near the eastern end of Pearis Mountain, where the land is cleaved by the New River Valley.

On my final day, as I descended the steep trail down the mountain, with a scheduled rendezvous with Diane in Pearisburg, for a ride home, I came face to face at one switchback with Richard, wearing a matching ballcap. He was feeling better, and had decided to join me for the hike into Pearisburg.

By early summer of 1997, I decided to hike a new section of the Tonto Trail within the Grand Canyon in November. I would do the Bass-Hermit loop, an 8 day hike including the western portion of the Tonto Trail. My mother, living in St. Louis, thought that was a crazy idea for a man who had a heart attack the previous year. Perhaps it was, but I was feeling more confident in my steadily improving endurance.

Micah and I drove out to the Grand Canyon from Virginia, and spent the night before the hike in the large campgrounds on the South

Rim. The temperature dropped well below freezing, as we camped in our tents. The following morning, an off-duty park ranger (by prior arrangement) drove us out the horrid, dirt road to the South Bass trail head, and wished us luck.

I had spent many hours investigating the smallest of details about that planned trek, and carried a list of water sources (usually reliable in November, but a suicidal quest during the summer), and felt comfortable about the distances to be hiked each day. Meals were carefully decided, based on calories and carry weight. I believe my pack weighed in at about 40 pounds with 6 liters (12 pounds) of water included.

The weather and temperatures turned out to be perfect for backpacking. Many of the trails were steeper than I had anticipated, especially excursions down side canyons, to reach the Colorado. The most difficult day for me was the climb-out of Hermit canyon to the South Rim. I just took my time, with Micah reaching the Rim long before I did. The sight of the parking lot at Hermit's Rest was a sweet moment.

Micah and I had now traversed the Tonto Trail—in two separate trips—from near its western end, at the South Bass Trail intersection, all the way to Indian Garden at the Bright Angel Trail intersection.

On returning home (out-running another blizzard, this time between New Mexico and Missouri), I immediately began to plan a hike of the eastern section of the Tonto Trail. That seemed too "short", so I included the Escalante Route, which originates at Tanner beach, and winds (and climbs and dives) westward to reach the Tonto Trail, which then continues westward to the Bright Angel Trail at Indian Garden. It would be a 10 day trek. I invited others to join me.

The planning was daunting. I made up checklists for required and suggested gear, as well as food, stove and shelter suggestions. What temperatures to expect and prepare for. How much water capacity to carry, how much stove fuel. I obtained backcountry reservations for a party of 6. In the end, 5 of us would do the hike over Christmas of 1998—three experienced and two inexperienced backpackers.

In as much as the difficulty of the trail—the Escalante Route in particular—was challenging for the experienced backpackers, I should have either not invited less experienced hikers, or modified the planned trek.

With our frigid night of camping at the South Rim fresh in my mind, I reserved a room for all 5 of us at Maswik Lodge for that night before the hike. The roads were well plowed of snow, but the trails were not. Starting on the upper Tanner Trail, each of us wearing securely attached, buckle-on instep crampons, we walked on an icy, snow-covered treadway as far as the lower cliff of the Coconino and the sloping, upper Supai, before dropping below the snow level. It allowed some truly wonderful photographs. For the rest of the day, and the remainder of the 10-day hike, perhaps with the exception of the climb-out through the upper Bright Angel Trail, we would keep our instep crampons in our packs. When there is no ice, those instep crampons feel like a soda can crimped onto the bottom of each boot.

All along the Escalante Route, which the Park Service considers wilderness, tent camping is "at large". You pick your own place to camp, and just set up your tent. Once we reached the Tonto Trail, then we would be constrained by the backcountry permit to camp only at the sites designated on the permit.

Like other "wilderness" trails (perhaps the quotes should surround the word, "trail"), the Escalante is sometimes difficult to locate, and is loosely woven with alternative paths. There are no trail markers, other than an occasional cairn (a little stack of rocks) left by some previous hiker. Having read a number of trek logs of hiking the Escalante, I knew in advance that in some areas, the right way is always just a good guess. In quite a few stretches of the Escalante, it is not humanly possible to hike anywhere but along the correct path.

On our third hiking day, we climbed out of Escalante Canyon, climbed up and over a steep ridge of loose scree, and down the other side. Most of the rest of the day's hike would be out at the very edge of the Tapeats cliff, at the verge of the Inner Gorge. Then we would follow the eastern rim of Seventy-Five-Mile Canyon to reach its creek crossing, where we would then descend into floor of the canyon, and make camp on the beach at the Colorado.

Micah and I were well out ahead of the others that day, with Micah well ahead of me. So each of us encountered this hiccup as a solo backpacker. It was along that eastern rim of Seventy-Five-Mile, about half way to the creek crossing. There was a seep a few feet above the treadway.

Seeps in the Grand Canyon are the emergence of water where no flowing creek exists. Water (usually from precipitation on the Rim) penetrates the crumbled layers of rock, and flows downward through the rock, until it encounters an impermeable layer. Then the water flows along that layer, emerging above ground only where the edge of impermeable stone has been eroded away.

Night temperatures had been below freezing inside the Canyon, but warmed during the day to comfortable, jacket wearing temperature. This particular seep, just to the upside of the treadway, had been in the shadow cast by the high ridge we had just crossed over. When we reached it, it was just beginning to see direct sunlight. So the water seeping over the trail partially froze, as it flowed over a three-foot stretch of trail, on its way into the side canyon.

When I reached the seep, and saw the three-foot span of ice in my path, I briefly considered removing my pack, and bringing out my instep crampons—to strap on, walk three feet, then unstrap and return them to my pack. I decided to take a generous, leaping step. I just barely found footing on clear trail as I landed from my leap.

It was only then, with my heart pounding a bit at the fact that I had almost landed on the icy part, that I gave any thought to what I had just done. I had been walking along the very edge of a 700 foot cliff for the past hour, and had been mildly relieved walking at the edge of a drop of merely a few hundred feet. Even without the ice, a misplaced step too far to the right would have sent me down a 70° slope of loose rock, which ended in a 300 foot vertical drop to the floor of Seventy-Five-Mile Canyon.

Micah's recollection of the seep is similar, with the difference being that he had considered the possible consequences in advance, fretted first, then made the leaping step.

32. Down to the Tonto Trail—the Rock Slide

1998

The trek logs that I had read about Papago Creek, another hurdle on the Escalante Route in the Grand Canyon, made clear that there were two serious challenges in climbing out of Papago, then descending to Red Canyon, the eastern terminus of the Tonto Trail. But their descriptions were vague, and seemed to differ on the routes chosen.

There is no trail or path westward out of Papago Canyon. There is just a raggedy, stair-step cliff that must be climbed, hand over hand, without wearing a pack. The pack must then be roped up to the next higher stair-step. In planning the trek, I worried most about this cliff. I purchased 100 feet of static line (used by rock-climbers), and carried it in my pack, just in case. I never used it.

The cliff was indeed difficult for all of us, but not as bad as I had imagined. Somebody had left cairns at critical decision points. And on reaching the top, I realized that I had never really felt exposed during the climb. Wow! All that worrying for nothing much.

At the top of Papago's western cliff, a conspicuous path wandered among enormous boulders, but remained mostly level. We were almost to Red Canyon, another night's sleep, and a morning start on the Tonto.

Then came the sudden and sobering view of the slope we would have to descend in order to reach our destination for that day. Surely we had missed a turn somewhere. But this was the notorious rock slide, described in inadequate detail in the trek logs.

The rock slide is a thirty-foot wide path that descends several hundred feet of elevation. But it is improbably steep. I would guess that its slope is greater than 70°. To my eye, it is steeper than the angle of repose for the boulders that are strewn all over it. They should just tumble on down at the lightest touch. These boulders are not the smooth stones we see at river rapids. They are sharp and angular blocks of stone. Many are the size of a truck, and rest at a scary tilt.

Worse, the only reasonable path for a hiker carries him or her beneath some of those overhanging, tipped, truck size boulders. Since the majority of the slope of the rock slide consists of small, loose stones, it is not possible to take simple steps. Each footfall is followed by a (hopefully) short downward slide, as the scree gives way. Because of this instability of footing, each hiker must place a hand against at least one of the tipping boulders in order to pass beneath its overhang.

I easily envisioned a touched boulder resuming its trip down the rock slide, and crushing me to a bloody smudge in the process. Unlike the Papago cliff, the rock slide did not offer a simple way to rope a pack downward. Most of us descended while wearing our loaded backpacks.

Even with the most careful steps, at least a few smaller rocks were sent careening all the way to the bottom. As a precaution, only one hiker descended the entire length of the rock slide at a time. One by one, we watched from the top or the bottom, as the other members of our party successfully made their way, ever so slowly, to the bottom. Only one member required some assistance part-way down.

Did any of us almost die? None of those huge, truly frightening boulders budged at all. But each of us sent rocks down the slope, and each of us slipped at least a few inches with nearly every step.

What I find hard to imagine is trekkers who have actually gone in the opposite direction—ascending the rock slide to Papago. I suppose it would be a process of two steps climbing up, one step sliding down. I would never attempt it, and would not like to descend the cliff into Papago Creek.

One member of our party noted, on reaching the bottom of the rock slide, that it was the scariest thing he had ever done in his life. But he did it!

33. Comware Computers Retreat—the Zip Line

1999

My brother, Richard's computer business had grown, in the computer-savvy, early-adopter, Blacksburg community that surrounded Virginia Tech. I now managed an increasing number of employees, many of whom were college age or under.

With the thought of improving our service and performance as a business, Richard planned a company retreat. It would be a team-building experience, and one that solicited and discussed new ideas and proposals. The retreat was held in a purpose-built, small resort in the northern Virginia forests.

There were organized, physical cooperation exercises designed to engender trust among the participants. There were nature walks and group conferences. One such conference session focused on the then popular trend of constructing a brief but comprehensive mission statement—the core purpose of the business. The resulting mission statement would serve as an anchor point for future business decisions.

Mission statements are analogous to the preamble of the US Constitution—inspiring, encompassing, airy—and often promptly forgotten. I recall a heated debate over the concluding phrase, "providing w, x, y and z for all." Did it really need the "for all" appendage? What did "for all" add, that would be lost from the ultimate meaning of the mission statement if it were not added? As one might guess from my recounting of this process, I was then and remain now a skeptic of the value of a mission statement, other than for purposes of verbose marketing.

But I enjoyed spending non-work time with everyone there. The setting was lovely, the meals enjoyable, and the lodging accommodations comfortable.

During my USAF water survival training at Homestead Air Force Base, near Miami, one of our training exercises required us to climb the uncountable steps up a tall tower, at the top of which a steel cable was attached. The cable descended across a body of water, and anchored to a post on the other side. The purpose of this zip line was for the trainee, me, to attach my parachute harness to the trolley (the pulley), jump off, then release the harness attachments at a safe distance above the water. I then splashed into the water, and swam out. The notion was to be able to release a real parachute from its harness, before landing in the ocean, in order to avoid being covered and enveloped by a wet nylon canopy.

Zip lines became popular all on their own, as a tourist attraction. A tourist can sail high above a forest, expending no muscle energy, then safely descending a tower at the far end.

At our retreat, we lined up for their zip line one afternoon. In contrast to the USAF water survival zip line, which relied on me to release at the proper time, this entertainment version incorporated a speed brake of sorts. The braking mechanism determined how fast the tourist traveled, and was supposed to be set by the operator according to the body weight of the tourist. This would allow the zipping human to gently slow to a halt at the end of the cable.

When my turn to strap in arrived, I was asked my body weight, and replied honestly. The brake adjustment was made as quickly as flipping a light switch.

I soared through the tree tops at an ever accelerating speed. It did not feel safe. As I neared the massive pole to which the far end of the cable was anchored, I immediately realized that I would smack into that pole and its assorted fixtures at high speed. I curled my body, and lifted both my legs high, so that my feet would impact the pole first. Even with that precaution, the collision knocked the wind out of me, and left me with a pulled muscle in my thigh. My feet hurt, but my body and head were still intact. Mission statement: to entertain, and not kill our guests.

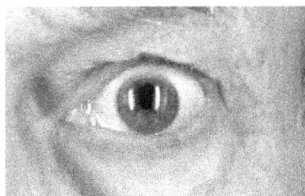

34. Stroke of Luck at Age 61

2009

After surviving my self-treated heart attack in 1996, my probability of dying within the following 12 months was about 50%. Not great odds. I did everything I could to rehabilitate my heart and my body. But somehow, when I solo-hiked in the Grand Canyon in 2001, my body weight was up to 212 pounds (on my 5'8" frame). During my climb-out, the expressions on the faces of folks who passed me as they hiked down suggested to me that I looked worrisome to them.

My solution was to purchase clothes in larger sizes, and to not worry too much about it.

When I hiked the Canyon again in 2006, this time with a small group, I encountered similar responses as I climbed out. "Are you alright?", strangers would ask. I was the last of our group to reach the rim that day. The fact that I reached it at all seemed to me to be a satisfactory cardiac stress test.

Once I finally chose to put my health care into the hands of a physician other than yours truly, the picture of my health became clearer. Assorted imaging and lab studies were performed, and all showed that my health was at risk from a number of simultaneous problems. I'll defer a tedious recounting here of the status of my various organs. I was resistant to adding more medications to my ever-growing list. My physician's most powerful words in response were, "I really hate to say it, but...diet and exercise."

It was shortly after that moment of seeing the light that I experienced a migraine headache one evening. I had had occasional migraines since my twenties. (Only in my late 60s did I realize that consuming ethanol—a beer, a glass of wine or a shot of whiskey—was one of my migraine's most consistent triggers.)

I don't remember if I had consumed any ethanol that day, but the right side of my head pounded. I took some Phenergan with codeine, and went to bed in the early evening. I didn't awaken until mid-morning the following day.

I promptly noticed that my left arm and leg felt partly "asleep". But unlike other occasions, when I have slept on top of my arm, the paresthesia did not fade after I had gotten up and moved around. On top of that, those two left extremities felt weak. I became concerned.

One test of neurologic function is to touch in rapid succession the tip of the thumb to the tip of each finger on that hand. My right hand worked just dandy. But the fingers of my left hand seemed to lack some of their normal movement. I was unable to make Spock's "Live long and prosper" hand signal. The intrinsic muscles of my left hand were notably weak. Those are the muscles that spread the fingers apart and draw them back together.

I went to the bathroom mirror, and studied my face. Both my pupils reacted to a bright light normally, but my grin was now asymmetrical. And that side of my face felt slightly numb to my touch.

Like the fool that I was with my heart attack, I did not seek medical attention. I knew that I had experienced a stroke the evening before, and had slept through those golden hours. By mid-morning, my neurologic deficits were stable (i.e. not progressing).

The most immediate consequence of this stoke was that I could no longer play classical guitar. My left hand just couldn't fret the strings—nylon strings. Mercifully, my ability to type was only minimally impacted, and has improved since. Between 2009 and 2011, I constantly had the impression that my cognition was not a sharp as it had been.

As a remedy to my brain fog, I started taking college level courses on-line, through Coursera.org, starting with Andrew Ng's *Machine Learning*. By the time I stopped taking every interesting Coursera course I came across, I had completed 27 of them.

So my lovely Swedish-made Goya classical guitar now hangs on my living room wall as a decoration.

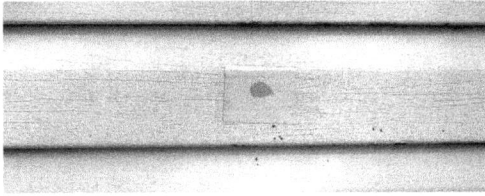

35. Holes in My House

2011

It was a beautiful autumn afternoon. I sat on the front porch of my old farmhouse. Puffs of a cigar punctuated the writing on my laptop computer. The pasture that extends 100 yards from my porch had recently been mowed for the third time, and its resulting huge, round bales of hay carried away to my neighbor's barn.

Both summer and winter, I spend a significant portion of my time sitting on my front porch, working on my computer, smoking a cigar, sipping coffee in the morning, or cold, well water later in the day. I frequently gaze over the top of my reading glasses, scanning the pasture and the sky above it. That two-acre pasture slopes gradually upward, to embrace two brick homes, just before reaching the eastern continental divide. [Piss on my side, and it goes into the Gulf of Mexico. Piss on the other side, and it heads for the Atlantic Ocean.]

This same, open porch (from which I am writing this book) is my observation platform for listening, and watching rabbits, voles, moles, squirrels, chipmunks, opossums, raccoons and ground hogs scampering, both day and night. Whitetail deer regard my yard and the adjoining, partially fenced pasture as a safe zone. I talk to them frequently, as I also do with the dozens of bird species that sing and bicker and harass one another every day. The porch is also my own safe zone.

When I heard a crisp cracking noise from somewhere close-by, on that lovely autumn afternoon, my first impression was that the cheap vinyl siding on the house had made an abrupt, thermal realignment, as the sun swept out of its view.

I heard it a second time, but apparently from the back of the house. This was clearly abnormal. But the third occurrence was different. I clearly perceived a higher pitch whoosh or whistle preceding the crack. And this time, I saw a new hole in the vinyl siding beside the porch. On the fourth, the clink of a cracked window pane toward the rear of the house. *Small-caliber gunfire!*

Walking down the four porch steps, and out into the yard allowed me to hear the direction from which the bullets were coming: from just over the rise to the south.

Trusting in the big sky theory, I walked to my parked car, started it, and drove the circuitous half-mile to reach the aging, three-story farmhouse that I knew to be situated over that rise. I rolled my car up the dirt driveway, and on to its back yard, where I could see four young men standing—one holding a .22 caliber rifle. They seemed surprised by my arrival.

Between them and my nearby, over the horizon house, an entire deer carcass hung from an ancient white oak tree. The scenario become instantly clear.

"We were just having some target practice with that deer."

I did not express anger, but rather their need to consider safety, when shooting a firearm. Their weapon could easily fire a bullet a half-mile or more, yet they had not taken the trouble to walk 30 yards, in order to see what might be on the receiving end of their target practice.

These were four brothers, the oldest of whom appeared to be just barely in his 20s. They had recently rented the house, and were now living there. All of them apologized. I couldn't help but wonder who had introduced them to guns, yet had failed to provide them with adequate gun safety education.

On returning home, I inspected each of my building structures with a surface facing the carefree gunfire. I found two holes in the vinyl siding of the house, two embedded .22 short bullets in the wall of my oak-plank shed, and a small bullet hold through the window of that shed. No hole in the side of my head that faced in the same direction.

36. In the Bathroom During a Lightening Storm

2012

I've mostly avoided taking a shower during an active lightning storm. That just seems obviously dangerous. But what I consider an "active lightning storm" is something of a blur.

For the safety of my laptop computer, I disconnect it from wall power if there is thunder nearby, or lightning visible within several miles. One unfortunate strike on an electrical power line down the road can surge the electric current enough to easily fry the delicate electronic components on the motherboard. When I was still managing Comware Computers, in Blacksburg, I replaced many a computer that had thus been fried. A decent surge suppressor will prevent those kinds of electrical surges, but not a direct strike on a house's wiring. For that, only being unplugged at the time of the strike will preserve a piece of electronics.

The sad reality is that a lightening strike 15 to 20 miles away, farther away than the sound of thunder can travel, may cause injury and death. But I have to assume that those "expert" pronouncements are what is *possible*, rather than what is *likely*.

I have often sat out on my front porch at night, watching lightning storms pass by. It's beautiful, as are the towering, cumulonimbus clouds. I count the seconds between the flash and the rumble, and estimate 1 mile ever 6 seconds. If a strike seems to be less than a couple of miles, and moving closer, then I go inside the house. And a strike that is so close that it makes me jump—well, that's always a good moment to go indoors.

One afternoon, an unimpressive thunderstorm was moving nearby. It approached while I was sitting on the toilet in my old farmhouse. My feet were on dry floor. My butt rested against a plastic seat. I was touching no plumbing fixtures. No worries.

When done, I went to the bathroom sink to wash my hands. I ran the water onto my hands, lathered them with Ivory bar soap, and lifted them beyond the stream of running water. Crack!

Lightning struck somewhere so close that I heard the deafening clap of thunder instantaneously. Much more worrisome was that I saw a bright spark leap from the outlet of the sink faucet to the metal rim at the sink drain. My lathery hands had been about to plunge into that very stream of water, for a good rinsing.

It took about ten seconds for the muscles in my arms and shoulders to relax enough to even consider going ahead now to rinse the soap from my hands. I'll just say that it was a quick rinse.

I stepped over to the towel rack, beside the toilet, and dried my hands. Only then did I recall having been sitting on that toilet moments before, with my genitals dangling precariously close to the water in the bowl. The sink spark had jumped the 8 or 9 inches between the faucet and the drain, appearing to ignore the stream of water. Had I been 8 or 9 inches from some grounding points while seated on the toilet? I shuddered to contemplate it.

Surely at the sink, a high-voltage spark to both wet hands could easily have traversed my electrolyte-filled arms and chest, administering a jolt to my heart. They might eventually have found my fully clothed body dead on the bathroom floor. But getting zapped while seated on the toilet suggests a different scene greeting the coroner.

37. John Deere vs. Dwarf Winesap

2021

I lovingly planted them as tiny saplings. I protected and nurtured them for over two decades. This was my second orchard. In the early 2000s, I put in plums and peaches and nectarines and pluots, apricots, prunes, cherries pears and sever varieties of apples. These were joined by raspberries, blackberries, blueberries, red grapes and green grapes.

The fruit trees, I regularly pruned—a late winter activity involving the hauling out of my stepladder, loppers and pruning saw. I would study the branch angles and always carefully prune just beyond a downward facing bud. They were tidy, sturdy fruit trees, with properly spread branches.

Year by year, one or more of them would die. Some I replaced; some not. By 2021, I had only two pear trees, two apple trees, both grapes and my blackberries. The two dwarf pears had surreptitiously bypassed their dwarfing rootstocks, and subsequently grew into full size pears, which produce massive quantities of delicious pears about once every three years. They are now way too tall for me to seriously prune them, since my stepladder skills are diminished by old age.

Eventually, I could no longer prune the two surviving apple trees—a yellow delicious and my cherished Winesap. They would have to make due on their own, with the burden of their branches and fruit.

During my annual pruning, I would make sure that any lower branches that might interfere with mowing on the lawn tractor were removed completely, leaving only the sturdy wood that I had trained to support the fruiting branches. But like my own body, time gradually, almost imperceptibly causes sagging. My increasing kyphosis (the hunching of my spine that forces me to sometimes walk with my knees partly bent, in order to continue my defiance of gravity) is reflected in the sturdy, central branches that make up my aging fruit trees. Each summer, those thick branches, which were once angled upward at about 60°, sag a little closer to the horizontal.

During the summer of 2021, I found that I had to dip my head and shoulders down to pass beneath the canopy of the Winesap while seated on my ancient John Deere lawn tractor. What was not apparent to me was that, as the fruit enlarged, those sagging, Winsap branches inched their way lower.

In the autumn, while mowing beneath that tree, I lowered my upper torso against the John Deere steering wheel, and tipped my head off to the side away from the trunk, just as I had done all summer long. I crept at the slowest forward speed I could maintain. But this time, I found my shoulders entrapped by an interlocked nest of nearly inflexible branches. Chest against the steering wheel, head tipped over to the side away from the two foot pedals that determine whether I am going forward or reverse, I lifted my somewhat floppy right foot, sight unseen, to place it onto the reverse pedal.

The John Deere lurched forward about 6 inches. I heard cracking of branches. I heard cracking of my neck. My hands and legs instantly felt an electrical-like surge. I was immediately certain that I had finally completed that partial cervical displacement from my unfortunate hecht vault over a half-century earlier.

I carefully reversed the John Deere, to extricate myself from beneath the tree, then stopped, to reach for my cell phone. Nope. I never carry the cell phone when mowing. My neck felt horrible, I felt slightly nauseated, but my extremities were still functioning.

Taking great care to keep my neck upright and stable, I slowly drove the John Deere back to its shed, and cautiously walked back to the house. Inside, I improvised a neck brace from a strip of closed-cell foam and bandanas. Then I sat out on my porch, deciding what to do next. Should I just call an ambulance? Should I be patient, and see how it changes?

I believe that my decision to just wait was a combination of feeling awful, but still able to move my arms and legs as usual, together with being exhausted as well as filthy from mowing for the previous two hours. [Physicians are always terrible patients.] I didn't eat dinner that evening, but did drink some broth. I was not confident that this accident would turn out well.

That night, I slept flat on my back, no pillow, and with the improvised neck brace in place. Muscle spasms in my neck were painful. Any movement of my neck produced a sickening, crunching sound.

I arranged an appointment at the VA clinic (it would be a few days), purchased a real neck brace, and endured the neck pains and facial bruising that slowly appeared. Simple activities were nearly impossible, like reaching to the side of the toilet, to tear off some toilet paper. I could not look down to untie or tie my boots. While driving, I could not rotate my head at all. I discovered that I cannot fold a t-shirt without trapping it beneath my chin.

Eventually, the neck CT scan at the VA hospital showed no increased displacement of that hinky neck vertebra, but to my eyes (not those of the radiologist) the overhanging, anterior lip of that vertebra appeared a bit crisper, more clearly defined than on previous studies. My guess is that during the initial impact, that subluxation slipped toward my spinal cord, tweaking my arms and legs in the process, then settled back into its long-time location—a more stable position. Another inch or two of forward motion by the John Deere would likely have resulted in quadriplegia as the best outcome.

I wore a neck brace for a couple of months. Altogether, I experienced some degree of neck pain and limitation of neck motion for about four months afterwards. As I write this, about eight months after my encounter with the Winesap, my neck is back to its previous, creaky self, and causes no more pain than the rest of my crooked back. It was way more than a sprain, and way less than dead.

As I grow older and older, my penchant for risky activities is subdued by my physical limitations. So, hopefully this neck business will be the end of my list of situations that could have gone either way.

37. Epilogue

25 June 2022

My original plan for this final vignette of the book was to carp on climate change, and how civilized man has signed its own, irrevocable death warrant—that it can go only one way now.

But a back ache awakened my 74 year-old body today while it was still dark outside. Somehow, in the blur of my sleepy mind, I recalled having checked the forecast for this morning, to decide if it would be too cloudy for something. Cloudy? Something? The planets! Would it be worth getting up at 5:00 am to look for the alignment of the planets in the predawn sky! The forecast had predicted 25% cloud cover.

I checked the clock. 5:00 am. I dressed in the dark (don't want to spoil that night vision), then groped around my back porch for my headlamp that can shine a red-only beam. I put on a sock hat and a thick fleece vest, since I never know how chilly it might be at 5:00 am. In the darkness, I went outside, averting my gaze from the scattered insecurity lights of neighbors, and walked out toward the paved road. I was over-dressed for the lovely, 60°F morning.

Half-way down my driveway, an unseen raccoon growled at me from one of the big maple trees in my front yard. I growled back, and continued to the road. It must have been that unblinking, red eye staring at him that encouraged the raccoon to concede this particular confrontation. The sky was mostly clear, in a soft shade of predawn blue. There were patchy areas of barely discernible haze.

I immediately identified Venus and the fingernail Moon. Jupiter was obvious, but Mars was missing. And I did not have a clear view of the sky where Saturn should have been. Almost directly overhead, the unmistakable, steady light of sun reflecting from the solar panels of the International Space Station slowly cruised from zenith toward the northeast. Looking directly at Venus, I could detect a faint presence where Mercury should be. Only the planetary alignment, and the exact knowledge of where it should be allowed me to be confident about it.

Even though Mars and Saturn were missing in action (one behind haze, the other behind towering trees), I wish to thank my back ache for getting me out of bed at the proper time on a stunning, summer morning.

This sky map has to show the interior of a spherical dome, so the planets appear on a curve. In reality, they were stretched out along a nearly straight line.

Sitting on my front porch, I sip on a mug of black coffee, puff a delicious cigar, and squint into the morning sun, as I type this final page.

END

www.ingramcontent.com/pod-product-compliance
Lightning Source LLC
LaVergne TN
LVHW011407080426
835511LV00005B/419